Sending BIG

Marc with a "C"

HOPE from the HEREAFTER

Joy Elaine Reed

Joy Elaine Reed

Marc with a "C"

HOPE
from the
HEREAFTER

Prompted by Her DEPARTED SON Who Unknowingly Overdosed on Fentanyl, This Psychic Medium Shares His Comforting SIGNS and MESSAGES From the AFTERLIFE.

JOY ELAINE REED

Joy Elaine Reed

Copyright © 2022 by Joy Elaine Reed

All rights reserved. No part of this book may be reproduced in any form or by any means or transmitted by any mechanical, photographic, or electronic process, or by photocopying, or in the form of a phonographic recording; nor may it be stored in a retrieval system, transmitted, or otherwise be copied for public or private use - other than "fair use" as brief quotations embodied in articles and reviews - without prior written permission of the author. For permission requests, email the author directly at the email address: joyelainereed@gmail.com

Cover Design: Art infinity book cover designer

Emails and notes were reprinted with the permission of the authors.

The author of this book does not dispense medical advice or prescribe the use of any technique as a form of treatment for physical, emotional, or medical problems without the advice of a physician, either directly or indirectly. The intent of the author is only to offer information of a general nature to help you in your quest for emotional, physical, and spiritual well-being. In the event you use any of the information in this book for yourself or others, the author assumes no responsibility for your actions.

To protect the privacy of others, certain names and details have been changed, and certain characters and events have been reordered or compressed.

ACKNOWLEDGMENTS

The greatest thank you in my heart goes to God for giving me this life to live and for blessing me so abundantly. Thank You for constantly guiding me in the right direction, allowing me to accomplish my life's purpose and write Marc's book. I am so humbled by my awesome blessings and my inspired life.

A super huge thanks to Spirit and Marc for giving me the words that are in our book and the courage to write our story. You blew me away with your constant directions and text!

I thank the love energy of the Beyond for their sweet guidance and words: Pap and Gram, this book would not have been possible without you and I love you so. I am your baby, Marc is my baby, and the book is Marc's baby! Thanks for wanting me to be your baby!

I especially want to thank my loving husband and editor Denny Reed, and I am so grateful that he taught English for 40 years. What a gift of insight and patience you gave to me as we worked together. Our love and my gratitude are eternal. God knew what was good when He/She brought us together in love. Kisses and hugs to you always.

Thank you to my sweet caring family who related stories, sent pictures for me to share, and kept me on the right track, while always loving me: Adam, Brittany, Shelley, Christopher, Nancy Reed, Roxanne Janosik, Joannie Tutin, and Lori Schafer. Thanks for your love and kindness, and direction. I am so grateful that we are souls united as a family. It's all good!

A thank you from the depths of my heart to my soul sister Zee Williams, who sat on the sofa with Marc in spirit and ate popcorn while they watched my zany and wild Book-Birthing show. Thanks for laughing at my anxiety, for putting my head back on my shoulders, and for bringing me back to earth more times than I can count during my incredible writing journey.

A special thanks to my intuitive Soul Truth Tribe, who gave me invaluable insight and Aha moments and constantly filled my life with love and amazing messages: Christina O'Brien, Christine Jette, Katie Rose, Stephanie Hall, and Austin Brodt, and the BYOT gals.

To my computer wizard and "third son", Jimmy Rogers, I offer my heartfelt thanks for your patient instruction and understanding. You're the greatest gentleman and teacher ever!

Many thanks to my author friends and book gurus who gave me the knowledge and direction that enabled me to get this book out to the world: Rick Buker, Romana Gould, Dan Piocquidio, Art infinity book designer, and especially my sweet and dear friend across the sea - Sean Graham… you're absolutely the very best of the best. Kudos to you!

Thanks to all our wonderful family of friends who are my blessings, helpers, and cheerleaders, and who helped make this book a reality: Loretta Orr, Linda Bartoy, Don Bartoy, Pamella Cobb, Eric Riggins, Susan Walker, Stan Miller, Matthew McCann, Diann Giles, and Dotty McKenna. Sending big love to you all.

And, most importantly, a heartfelt thanks to YOU for reading our book. We want you to heal. You are the reason we have all come together. Thanks so much for being you! You are an amazing blessing throughout the Universe. I am sending big love to you always and keeping you in my thoughts and daily prayers.

DEDICATION

This book is dedicated to Marc with a "C" who made this book a reality. We thank you for your sweet, caring soul and for bringing love into our lives wherever you may be. You showed us that love is all there is, and now we're ready to heal. Please continue to shine your light on us and the entire Universe. You've given us hope, and now you can rest in peace, honey. Sending Big Love to you for all eternity. Xoxoxo Mom

Joy Elaine and Marc with a "C"

Joy Elaine Reed

FOREWORD

YOU ARE READING THIS BOOK FOR A REASON

This is a true story that I send to you from the Hereafter. It's a gripping tale of psychological trauma, joy and gladness, hate and pain, love and kindness, and life and loss. In this book, you will experience a wild ride that includes unbelievable signs, messages, miracles, rainbows, swoops, dreams, love, gifts, and butterflies mixed with the murky heaviness of illness, suffering, bullying, tears, grief, hate, pain, gay-bashing, addiction, fentanyl, and murder. This is a fascinating true story of life, love, challenges, drama, and an untimely crossing over which ultimately leads to healing, hope, and acceptance.

This book is filled with many beautiful experiences of connecting to Spirit and psychic phenomena. Considering the psychic realm, you're either a skeptic or a believer. If you're a believer, you are awake. If you're a skeptic, you're intrigued. Either way, I assure you that this exceptional book came directly from me in another plane of existence where I reside since I have crossed over. I told my Mom what words to write. She's a psychic medium whom I talk with all the time, and I thank God that she can hear me! Mom is a Light Worker who connects with God and the angels. She wrote my amazing story because of my insistence, and she nailed it! I am so very proud of her for writing *MARC WITH A "C" - HOPE FROM THE HEREAFTER*. This was truly an outpouring of love on her part, for which I am so grateful. She listened to the uplifting words that Spirit and I gave her and typed her little fingers off! Kudos to Mom! She questioned this project for a long while but forged ahead anyhow. (I gave her no choice! I bugged the heck out of her!). Whether you're a skeptic or a believer doesn't matter. What matters are my assuring signs and words of hope to you. I want you to heal and go forward with love.

Joy Elaine Reed

As you know, you are not promised tomorrow. Now is the time to find soul truth
and peace.
    Grieving is a punishing process that is necessary to release sad energy from the body, mind, and Spirit. It's a process that turns hurt into healing. If you don't grieve, you won't heal. Healing doesn't happen overnight, and anything that can ease the pain is welcomed relief. Mom and I have met many people who have lost a child, a loved one, or a pet. Some of them cannot make their way out of their grief. They need to heal and find peace. This book has been written to bring you comfort, joy, and hope. When you can be grateful for, and celebrate the life of a loved one who has passed, your grief will lose its grip. The celebration of my life was Mom's inspiration for writing this book. Reading *MARC WITH A "C" - HOPE FROM THE HEREAFTER* may help you let go of pain and begin the healing process. It's time to celebrate the life of your son, daughter, mother, father, and all your departed loved ones and pets! You should be celebrating there on the earth plane because we're having one heck of a party over here! You can't believe the excitement here when another soul returns home! "Coming Home" is such a sweet celebration for us all.
    This book tells the remarkable story of healing the physical, emotional, and mental pain that physical death brings to those who remain. It's a story of freedom and peace. It's a story of truth and love with a happy ending.
    This is no "fluff piece", as Mom's retired English teacher husband calls some books he has read. This is a heavy-duty, life-lesson Spirit Textbook that tells of personal challenges and setbacks along with loving signs and messages from the Afterlife. My mission for Mom in writing this book is to give hope to those who have lost a loved one and are grieving. My family and friends have grieved for me, and I know that at times it was unbearable. But we on the
Other Side live on and want you to know that we are safe and we are helping you on your journey in life.
    We are not gone. Your pets are not gone. We exist in many other planes of awareness, where you do not live. The only thing that

separates us from you is a thin rainbow curtain of vibrational change. We don't want to see you cry over losing us. In the Hereafter, we are safe and we love you and will do anything it takes to give you that message. From the Other Side, we try to get your attention by sending signs to you. Our signs lessen the sting of grief.

Anything unusual or odd can be a sign… the lights may flicker, your electronics may go wonky, artwork on the wall may rattle (my personal favorite!), or your favorite song will play on the radio even if it's plugged in or not! Sometimes we leave feathers or coins for you to find. Our picture may pop up on your phone when we want to say hello. We love to take the shape of birds, too. You are not imagining things. Know that we are coming to you in Spirit, constantly trying to connect with your energy. That's a tough job for us. After reading this book, you will more clearly understand our motivation and perseverance.

I want you to know that everyone receives signs from the Afterlife. Observe. Listen. You may hear the voice of a loved one and you may think that you are losing your mind. It is quite unnerving! But, you're fine… you are just tuning into the Hereafter Channel. Enjoy your conversations with your loved ones, and notice the signs that they send to tell you that they love you and are always with you! My signs to Mom are included in this book to give you an idea of the unexpected happenings that can fill your heart with joy and peace.

Here's the essential message of *MARC WITH A "C" - HOPE FROM THE HEREAFTER,* and the message we send to psychic mediums who will tell you… "I am safe and better than I've ever been before. I am with you and I am helping you and I want you to know that I love you no matter what kind of relationship we had in our life together. I am sending you signs and messages to let you know that I'm at peace. And above all else, for all eternity, I am sending you my undying love.

Marc with a "C"

Eternal Universal Light Worker

Joy Elaine Reed

CONTENTS

PART ONE: INSPIRATION

GABBY- Page 3

GHOSTWRITER - Page 21

PART TWO: JOURNEY ON

BUTTERFLIES IN A YELLOW ROOM – Page 31

TOUCHY-FEELY – Page 37

BROTHERLY LOVE – Page 41

THE REAL WINNER – page 49

DARKENED ROOMS AND RAINBOWS - page 55

THE PRICE OF FREEDOM – Page 63

ANOTHER LIFETIME – Page 71

MARC WITH A "C" – Page 77

A GOOD PLACE – Page 85

ANGEL TALK – Page 91

SHANGRI-LA – Page 99

PART THREE: UNEDITED JOURNAL ENTRIES

BOBBY McGEE – Page 107

SO SURREAL – Page 119

AN AWESOME ANGEL – Page 127

FOOTPRINTS IN THE SNOW – Page 139

SENDING BIG LOVE – Page 147

SWOOPS – Page 157

POISON – Page 165

CHRYSALIS – Page 175

TIME IS AN ILLUSION – Page 189

LIGHT WORKERS – Page 199

BUBBLES OF LOVE – Page 209

THE ORANGE TOUR – Page 215

IT'S ALL GOOD – Page 219

PART ONE:

INSPIRATION

Joy Elaine Reed

CHAPTER 1

GABBY

On this chilly morning, as I sat mesmerized by the metronomic rhythm of the wipers on the wet windshield, I had no idea of the mystical journey that awaited me today and would change the entire direction of my life.

"Can you park closer to the front door?" I asked my husband as he pulled into a distant parking space at the medical facility. He had a thing about not parking too close to the front... handicapped or not.

I heard a loud sigh. "Geez, Joy. Why don't *you* drive from now on?"

Yep, there I was, giving Denny orders again, as I questioned my ability to maneuver my cane in this nasty, chilling downpour. *It would help if he parked closer to the door! Right now, I'm about as sure-footed as a one-legged ostrich wearing a chic ten-inch heel!* My loving husband had been such a compassionate caregiver to me thus far and assisted me during both my rehab and this ongoing recovery from my back surgery. I certainly appreciated him for being my chauffeur during these last six months. I was so thankful for everything he had done for me. Denny was my earth angel and soulmate, and I couldn't have made it this far without his help, and the unending help of all my wonderful family and friends. I realized that this morning, while I was having my scans performed inside this warm building, my husband would be patiently waiting for me as he sat outside in the frigid car and watched the rain bounce off his windshield. For obvious reasons, like seeing half-dressed women walking around wearing short blue mammogram tops, men weren't permitted to wait in the women's medical center. Then I felt sorry for him. I had to change the direction of my thoughts. I already knew that if I only focused on myself, it would prod my ego to fan open like a proud peacock's tail. *It's not all about me. I have to drop my ego and live my life caring about others.* I was grateful and I had to show it. Compassion struck the cords of my heart. I quickly apologized to Denny and said that the parking space he had chosen was just fine with me. Pondering as I unbuckled my seat belt, I blamed his cranky mood on driving me over here in the dark early morning pouring rain, and I assumed that my" Crankies" were a result of having no choice but to schedule a mammogram before noon. I had only one rule… I never scheduled anything before lunch. *I'm retired and have all the time in the world, but don't you dare mess with my mornings! Thank you very much. My lazy mornings are the sweet "me" part of my day. I am very protective of my "me time". I love these early morning appointments just about as much as I love driving seventy-five miles per hour in six lanes of traffic.*

During these past five days, the rain and the sun had been showing off as if they were in a dance competition. And, wouldn't you know? The rain won first prize. This fine state of Pennsylvania had a lot of good things going for it, but lovely weather wasn't one of them. *This is a far cry from the sunshine of the eastern seashore.* In Pennsylvania, mid-December offered a miserable mix of cold rain, snow, ice, or all of the above. It was difficult to differentiate the day from the night when the light of every single day seemed to begin at noon and end at dinner time because it was winter. *I can't believe that I am living back here again. Yuk. I'm so not used to this. Where's the sun? I NEED SUNSHINE!!! It's dark and wet here most of the time. I could grow mold while I sit here!* After just spending twenty wonderful sunny retirement years at the South Carolina shore, coming back to live in Pennsylvania again was still a shock to our systems. But Denny and I needed to be here now.

As the cold rain pelted me I did my best to swing my legs to the right and onto the ground as I slinked out of the bucket seat on the car's passenger side. Although I practiced this movement a million times in the rehab center's little blue wooden car, it was still challenging, and this downpour didn't help. *It wasn't raining when I learned this move in physical therapy! I don't want to fall down on my behind. Angels, please protect me and get me out of the car and into the building safely. I'm still iffy with my cane.* I pulled the hood of my coat up over my head so I wouldn't get drenched. Wobbling like a second-grade gymnast on the balance beam, I rose and grabbed the top of the car door with my left hand. In my other hand, I held my cane with a tight grip. *Here I go. Hope I make it.* I turned and wobbled toward the main door, taking particular care that my cane didn't slide out from under me on the slick sidewalk, although I trusted that the angels were guarding and protecting me. I waddled into the front door as if I were a penguin on slick ice.

The entrance to the women's health center opened into a large waiting room where eighteen masked ladies, dressed in heavy coats, sat three seats apart from each other in a forced effort to social distance. *Rain, pain, cane... and Covid. This year, 2021, is in so many unbelievable and crazy ways, entirely different for me now.* Pushing my hood off my head, I walked up to the registration desk. The receptionist looked at my doctor's orders for a mammogram and an ultrasound of my left breast. She pointed to the right and told me to sign in at the kiosk. I did as I was told, and then found a seat three chairs away from another woman. *We're all bundled up and masked as we quietly sit three chairs apart. This is weird. I feel as if I'm a programmed female robot stuck somewhere in a medical twilight zone with a ton of other robots. But, duh, if I'm a robot, I wouldn't need to social distance! Or get a mammogram!*

I waited, all the while wishing that I was at home relaxing and enjoying a cup of my husband's delicious coffee. I thanked the angels for their unceasing assistance and their constant guidance and protection. It felt good knowing that whenever I asked them for help, they took perfect care of me. *I am blessed to be surrounded by angels at all times. My team of angels and spirit guides provides me with super high-level security. They are truly the best and I dearly love them.*

To my surprise, in less time than it took to see if I had put my shoes on the right feet, a woman in a wash-out burgundy lab coat came through the double doors with a paper in her hand and loudly called out my entire name which echoed across the huge waiting room. *So much for confidentiality! Now that everyone here knows who I am, she might want to yell out my social security number and license number, too! HIPAA Laws, anyone? These are crazy times we're in now.* She led me down the hallway to a three-by-four-foot cubicle with a hamper and a locked wooden closet with a key for storing my clothing and valuables. She handed me a short blue heavy cotton top that "must open in the front" and told me to go to the small, ten-chair mammography waiting room when I was ready. *Ready? I don't think any woman is ever "ready" for a boob check. Yeah, I'm always ready to have my boobs smashed between two pieces of plexiglass! Seriously? This ain't a picnic.*

After I had tied the thick white cords of my anything-but-chic blue cotton cover-up, I walked across the hall to the small waiting room. The only person there was a petite woman seated in a chair. She wore a green fabric mask with little white polka dots and had on a blue top that matched mine. I took a seat across the room from her and noticed that she held the front of her top together with her hands, as she crossed her legs and pumped her right leg up and down. I felt her nervous energy bounce around her body. She looked at the television, but she wasn't watching the talk show. Her thoughts distracted her. As an evidential psychic medium, I sensed her sweet disposition and I knew that she was very concerned. Her energy was anything but calm.

"*SHE IS FULL OF FEAR*"... Spirit was speaking directly to me. I looked at the worried lady seated across the room. I was deeply pulled into her unsettled energy and knew that this woman dreaded being here for her mammogram. Because I am an empath who can feel the feelings of others, her fear hit me smack in the chest. My chest hurt as if I had a rope slowly tightening around my heart. *Please, God, give her peace and calm her mind.* I felt that she needed prayers. Most people do. Prayers worked when nothing else worked. *It feels good when I pray for others because it's a great way to get out of myself and ground my energy while I lift their vibration. Prayer is always a win-win.* So, I prayed for her.

I sat and looked around this sterile place where there was nothing to look at. I knew that I had no choice but to wait until they called for me. I have learned that patience, along with being a virtue, is a learned behavior. *I'm right where I am supposed to be now. I have no doubt that I'm here at the perfect time to be here. Patience, girl!*

In the past, playing the waiting game rocked my boat and aggravated me to no end. Waiting for anything always drove me crazy and ruffled my feathers! I always felt angry that someone was wasting my precious time. *How dare they? Don't they know just how important I am?* Then, one day I realized that my spirit guides and angels told me to tell my clients to be patient and that I, myself, wasn't paying a bit of attention to that message that I relayed to them. That's when I decided that I did, indeed, have a choice. I had the choice to change my feelings, which then changed my attitude about anything. I realized that if there was any situation that I could not change, at least I could change my feelings about what was happening. That was the only choice I could make. So I learned to ask myself, "Can you change this situation?" If the answer was "yes"… then I changed the situation, but if the answer was "no", then I changed the way I felt about what was happening. I looked for the good and ignored any bad stuff that I was experiencing. I made myself feel better about the situation because I knew that I had the choice to change my feelings. *My beliefs, thoughts, and feelings are the only things that I can change. Today, how I feel is up to me. I now choose to feel good. If I feel myself getting upset, I always say to myself…"This too shall pass. There's no need for me to get upset over something that I can't change.*

I knew that sooner or later, I'd be safe and at home while I sipped a cup of tasty and necessary coffee… and I smiled because

I deemed that cup of coffee to be my great reward for enduring this boob stuff. So I patiently waited and decided to talk to God, which is what I tend to do when I have alone time. *I love to talk and listen to the Universal Love Energy of Spirit.* *"Spirit" is my divine "team" composed of God, my spirit guides, all the angels and archangels, the saints, all the ascended masters like Buddha and Jesus, all my beloved loved ones who have "graduated", my totem animals, my nature friends, and my departed pet crew. Spirit is my higher power which I connect with daily so that I can receive divine guidance. It doesn't matter who or what I call my higher power, but it really, truly matters that I have one. It's essential for me to daily seek and connect with my powerful and benevolent creator of goodness and light, and all my other-worldly helpers.*

Connecting to Spirit changed my life. In the past, I had experienced a dark, grim state when each day of my life made me feel like I was the world's loneliest mountain climber. Every day I felt as if I were attempting a treacherous solo climb to the top of Mount Everest. Without equipment or oxygen, I struggled to reach the apex of that mountain. Higher and higher I climbed as the mountain got steeper and steeper. When I had finally trekked almost to the peak, I slipped and fell and tumbled to the bottom. Every day I felt like I had repeated the same climb and the same fall. There came a time when I had no more strength left in me, and I realized that I had a problem.

My problem was that I thought I was in control... of everything! *What an idea straight from hell.* For me, life became a crazy drama, and everything turned into a 911 in my head. My days were filled with panic attacks and digging through the garbage can until I got my hands on the stale, hard donuts that I had thrown away the night before. My life became like a runaway train flying down the track... with a bad ending looming close. *I'm falling apart! Lord, please put me back together! I am so broken.* I felt that I was losing control and no matter how hard I tried to keep it all together, control just kept slipping away. Like a buttered raw turkey, I couldn't hold on to it. Depressed and overweight, I thought that I was going to die, and I knew that I had to get professional help. I sought a therapist because I felt that I could not do this on my own. I was ready to truly experience and understand ME... the person who lived in this body that was a donut shy of busting the scales. I was deeply entrenched in the dark night of the soul. I had fallen to the bottom of the pit and could not crawl out without help. *It was only when I was all alone at the very bottom of that deep, dark ravine of depression that I could finally accept the fact that I did need expert help. I can't climb out of this pit of despair without someone to help me! I feel so alone and helpless!*

I became ready to look in the mirror and see the real me, but I was afraid of whom I might find staring back at me. I experienced extreme, heart-pounding fear when I was finally ready to see the true version of myself. I contacted a professional counselor to help me figure out the who, what, when, where, and why of me. I was finally doing something sane for the first time in my life. It was time for me to get real, feel, and heal. Over the years, with the help of many mentors, therapists, and healers, I eventually got my head out of my tush. I finally accepted the reality that I had control over nothing, so I let go of the idea that I was in control of everything. I turned the control of my life over to my higher power. My life flowed much better when I wasn't in charge of the world. I realized that I was never the center of the Universe, as I had thought!

Let me tell you, letting go was the toughest thing I ever did. I kicked and screamed until the day when I finally woke up. I eventually realized that giving up control of *everything* was a scary proposition, but since I had control over nothing, giving up control of *nothing* was less daunting. I was finally willing to let it all go, and I allowed someone or something else to be in charge. Today, I have nothing to control but my own beliefs, thoughts, and feelings. *Spirit is the center of my world, not me. I know that every single day, I must let go of my ego, and allow Spirit to lead me and work through me. In daily meditation, I visualize Spirit and myself riding a bicycle built for two. Spirit sits in front and turns the handlebars, while I sit in the back and pedal. I don't know where Spirit will take me, but I know that it's all good. I trust. For me, this works. Today I am happy.*

After a few minutes, another masked woman clad in the same short blue cotton cover-up joined us in the waiting room. As she walked past my chair, I felt her good energy, but she vibrated slowly and heavily. Because the whole world had now been programmed to social distance, she sat in the third seat down the row from me. *Everybody in the world is now programmed like Pavlov's dogs!* Through her mask, she said that she hoped her test would be done quickly, as she had to hurry back to work.

"ASK HER WHERE SHE WORKS"... I knew that Spirit was talking to me, so I opened my energy, listened carefully, and acted without question. "Where do you work?" I began the conversation as I smiled behind my face mask.

"The school bus." She offered.

I made an assumption. "Oh, I gotta give school bus drivers a ton of credit for what they do. You deserve five gold stars on your forehead. I was a teacher, but I could never do what you do. You guys are amazing."

"Oh, I'm not a driver. I ride the bus with the kids. I'm an aide on the bus assisting special needs students."

"ASK HER WHAT HER NAME IS"... I told her my name, and politely asked what her name was, and she shared that with me. I have a thing about names. I've learned that all names have a special meaning, and it's a lovely sign of respect to call another by their given name. It piqued their attention and made for a beautiful soul connection. I always asked people for their names when we were engaged in a conversation or if they helped me in any way. *Names are important! They allow us to connect to the energy of that person. What would we all do without our names? Names become our identities. I am fascinated by names, and try my best to remember them, which is getting more difficult for me every day!!*

She told me that her name was Carol and she did, indeed, look like a Carol to me. *It's funny how people look like their names.*

"Oh, wow, Carol. Good for you. I used to teach kids with special needs."

"Really?" Carol's face lit up as her eyes smiled. "My daughter had special needs. She went to school at Bright Beginnings. Gabrielle is her name. Do you know her? I think everybody knew Gabrielle."

I saw this loving Mama Bear saunter out of her den as I said, "Well, I used to work at that school and her name sounds familiar. You know, I think I do remember her." I was unsure of knowing her daughter, but I instinctively knew that it didn't matter. I continued, "Do you know that the name "Gabrielle" comes from the name "Gabriel", who is one of my favorite archangels? Your daughter's name means "God is my strength".

Carol's face brightened as she smiled. "Gabby sure was my angel. Oh, she was something! She was a wonderful athlete and was in all the Special Olympics and won eight gold medals." Mama Bear beamed with pride. "She was a great runner, and she could long jump and sprint. She would leave the boys in her dust. She was amazing!" She took a quick breath. "She was prom queen, too, you know. Oh, that was such a magical night. Everybody said that Gabby was the prettiest prom queen that the school ever had. She looked so beautiful." She reached into the back pocket of her jeans and pulled out her phone. After tapping her screen a few times, she handed the phone to me. "Here's her picture. Do you think you remember her?"

I studied the photo. A stunning girl with a sweet smile glowed on the screen, wearing a midnight-blue sequined gown and a wrist corsage with pink roses. She looked more beautiful than any royal princess in any castle in any country. Carol's daughter was gorgeous with rich dark skin and blazing fireworks in her eyes. I read Gabby's energy from her photo… I could see that she was a loving girl full of joy and wonder. She had great vibes, but something was missing in her energy. It felt fractured, although, her broad smile showed how truly happy she was with her life. "Oh my, I do think I remember her. Wow, she's gorgeous. I can see that you're very proud of her as you should be. Heck, I'm even proud of her. Gabrielle's a wonderful girl." I spoke the truth.

Carol's eyes locked into mine. "Gabby died 5 years ago." She dropped her head down slowly and stared at the floor as the brightness left her face.

"*SHE IS STUCK IN GRIEF AND PAIN*"... That news crushed my heart as if I had just witnessed an out-of-control airplane spinning down out of the sky and crashing to the ground. *Oh, sweet Lord! How sad for her. Grief sucks!* "Oh, Carol, I am so sorry for your loss." As an empath, I felt her unrelenting pain as if I were living in her body, and I ached for her.

"Yeah. It's tough." Carol looked down at the dark brown multi-hued carpeting. "I mean, it's really tough. To lose someone as special as Gabby is unbelievable. That's why I help the kids on the bus because I feel I need to do this in memory of her. I'm trying to take away the hurt." As those feelings of pain left her lips, my entire being dived into a dark pool of heavy, deep sadness.

"*YOU ARE MY COMPASSIONATE LIGHT WORKER. I WILL GIVE YOU THE WORDS.*"... I was prompted to continue. "Aw, that's so sweet of you. I'm sure she appreciates your work with the other kids because I know how hard it must be."

"Yeah. Yeah, I do it for her." She sat and nodded her head.

I looked again at Gabby's photo. "Gabrielle is beautiful. Absolutely beautiful, just like you, Carol." My heart was beyond breaking for Mama Bear.

"*ASK HOW SHE CROSSED OVER. ALLOW HER TO RELEASE HER SADNESS*"... "May I ask how she passed?"

"She had kidney failure." She paused and looked up to keep the tears from trickling down her cheeks. "It's hard. I'm having a tough time. Nobody knows how horrible it is for me to try to go on every day without her." She let out a deep sigh. "I know it's been five years, but it doesn't get any easier. Nobody understands the emptiness of losing a child. It's just overwhelming pain and sorrow over and over again every single day."

"*YOU ARE A HEALER. SHARE YOUR STORY*"... As I handed back her phone I knew this wouldn't be easy for me. "I do understand, Carol." She turned and looked directly into my eyes with a "How would you know?" look. I continued, "My son died last December. It's been a year and two days." I swallowed my heartache as if it were a spoonful of liquid concrete about to harden in my throat. "I feel how you feel. I understand your pain."

In my life, even before Marc had crossed over, I'd known at least twenty parents who had lost their children. Carol was probably the fifteenth parent who had lost their child that I had met this past year since Marc died. *So many grieving parents are on this same journey with me.* I knew that in life, there were no chance meetings. I had become a magnet for grieving moms and dads. I guessed that Spirit saw my light and wanted me to shine it on these parents who grieve. But, what did I know?

Just then, a picture was "shown" to me......everyone on this whole round planet we called Earth seemed to be floating around in different-colored wooden rowboats on the same vast ocean! The ocean was boundless and the only thing that differed was all the colors of our rowboats. No two rowboats were the same color! *Everything's the same in our ocean except for the colors of our rowboats. Everyone's bobbing up and down in the same vast waters of life. The water is filled with joy and pain, grief and laughter, and every other feeling we will experience at one time or another.* I realized that there have been moments in our lives when every single one of us has had to grieve the loss of someone or something that we dearly loved, and I was now challenged to give this grieving lady a helping hand to heal her sorrow. I am a compassionate and loving empath, and I had to say the words that would pull Carol out of her pit of despair.

"YOU ARE SOUL SISTERS. LOVE ONE ANOTHER. SHARE YOUR EXPERIENCE"...I continued my tale, but it broke my heart to say the words... "Dear God, it was tough. Marc was my firstborn baby. When he died, I felt like mountain lions were ripping my heart out of my chest. There were days when my sobbing never ended. Those sobs came from so deep down in my throat. I had never cried that hard." I drew a deep, slow breath. "The pain is always here. It'll lessen, but I know it will always be a part of me - and a part of you. Nobody escapes grief. I hate it. It hurts so bad." *This hellish process is different for each one of us, and the "time" for grieving doesn't expire.* I swallowed the pain. "But life goes on. I know that I have to feel my feelings and then let them go. That's how grieving works for me. I feel the sadness. I cry and sob, empty a box of tissues, get up and walk out of the room, look out of the window, scream if I feel it, and then I let it go. When the sadness returns, I do it all over again because I have to release those feelings of sorrow. Each time seems to soften my feelings and make them less jagged. And that's comforting to me. I feel better when I release all my unhappiness and pain. Nobody should hold all that misery inside their hearts." *You can't shine your love light when you're filled with sadness.*

"IT'S TIME TO GIVE HER HOPE. TELL HER ABOUT THE CHRISTMAS LIGHTS"... "I can't believe Christmas is here again already. Boy, I had a super hard time putting up Christmas decorations this year." That was a difficult transition into the holiday mode but Spirit wanted me to talk with her about Christmas and, with Spirit, I do as I am told.

Carol laughed with her eyes closed. "I haven't put out any holiday decorations for the past five years. Why should I? I don't care about the holidays anymore. My house is dark." She paused, sighed, and continued. "My cousins and my sister live next to me on each side and tease me because my dark house is in the middle between their two houses. I swear that they have more glowing lights covering their yards and houses than you see at the airport. They decorate like crazy for Christmas, and I haven't done a thing since Gabrielle's death. I just can't bring myself to do anything for the holidays." She shook her head. "How can I celebrate when my sweet Gabby's gone?"

"NOW IS THE TIME TO HELP HER HEAL"... "Oh, honey, I know what you mean." I nodded. Knowing the healing power of a touch, I ached to lay my hand upon her hand, but that was a Covid no-no. "I don't even have an ounce of holiday spirit this year, but I do know that I'd feel really down with no Christmas decorations around at all. I know it's up to me to choose how I feel.

I have to deliberately make myself feel good, so I will keep going forward." I paused. "I gotta do something Christmas-y. I put up some lights and set a little tree right in the middle of my table. That was the best I could do, and I did feel a little better doing that. I have to try to be festive even though it hurts to breathe because of the heartache. Christmas carols are heart-wrenching to hear, so I can't listen to them now, but I know that one day I'll be ready. This awful time now is my new normal. And, I don't want it this way, but that's the way it is for now. It's a struggle, but I *need* Christmas. I need Christmas… and Valentine's Day… and Saint Patrick's Day… and Easter… and Thanksgiving. I need them all. I need to keep living. My Marc loved Christmas so much. This year I decorated a little bit for me and my husband, and for Marc, too."

The words that followed came out of my mouth like a swiftly flowing river… "He's not gone. He's home with me and my tiny tree and all the lights. I know he is. I hear his voice all the time, telling me and my husband that he is there with us. Marc wants to see us being joyful. I know he wouldn't be happy seeing his mother constantly sit and cry in a dark apartment. If I were where Marc is now, it would hurt me to look at him and see *him* crying over losing *me*. I know that there will be crying times, but he wants me to live in joy and gratitude as my life goes on. He wants me to celebrate his life, not his death. Marc loves everybody and wants to bring all people together as one. After he crossed over he told me to tell all his grieving friends that every time they see Christmas lights he wants them to think of him and smile as they remember all the good times they shared, and say a little prayer for him. He wants them to know that "It's all good". That's so like Marc — trying to make everybody happy. I'm sure that he's always with me, just as Gabrielle's always with you."

Carol reflected with a faraway look as she turned to face me. "She is?" I nodded and assured her. She paused and thought… "Ya know something? This is wild. Today, when I turned my phone on, Gabrielle's picture showed up on my screen. I was shocked! There she was! I just couldn't believe it." She pushed her hair behind her ears as she remembered.

"See what I mean?" I said as I smiled bigger than the Montana sky. "She was showing you that she's here with you. Carol, she gave you a sign that she loves you. She wants you to know that she's with you every minute of every day and that she is doing fine."

She reflected on my last statement. "Wow! That's something! Yeah, I think that I can feel her with me sometimes. I guess that's possible, right?"

"Absolutely. She's always with you. Just keep looking for those signs." I was so happy that I had reassured Carol. Being a psychic medium, I knew these things... over the years I have talked to many souls who had dropped their bodies, and I received countless signs and messages from them, telling me to tell their loved ones that "It's all good".

She paused and nodded again. "Oh, when I think back, I remember that every year I used to put lights all around our house and decorate a huge Christmas tree. Gabby loved hanging all the ornaments." Carol laughed as she reminisced and she made me smile. "Gabby hung every ornament on the front branches of the tree, and the sides and the back were bare!" She kept laughing and continued, "The tree looked so silly, but she was proud of her job. She had her favorite ornaments and got all excited with every single one that she lifted out of the box. Together we used to decorate the whole house for Christmas. Those were good times then. Once I remember hanging over twenty strings of lights outside. I used to do it good... no, *we* used to do it good. Gabby and I made Christmas at our house special."

"*GIVE HER A PEP TALK*"... "Could you hang some lights this year... for Gabby?"

"Oh, I don't know... I guess I could." She paused for a while in thought. "Maybe I could put a string of lights around the front window. Yeah. I could probably plug them in next to the front door." Gears in Carol's mind began to spin, as she visualized Christmas lights, windows, doors, and outlets. "I could even put a string of lights around the storm door for Gabby, too." Her positive thoughts brightened her energy. "I think I can put lights around my window in the dining room if I get an extension cord. Oh, Gabby would like that. She would want me to do that. She loved the colored lights... but not white lights... they had to be all different colors." *Just like our multi-colored rowboats on the ocean of life!*

I was so thrilled that her energy had quickened and I gave Carol a big grin under my mask. I wished that she could see my happy face. "Wow! It's like you just know exactly what Gabrielle wants you to do. I think that's great!"

She then spoke slowly and tried to convince herself. "Yeah, Gabby would like that." Carol nodded and began mentally planning her Christmas light schematics.

Just then, I was called to get my mammogram, so I left Carol with her plans and slowly walked to the imaging room. My energy was totally drained but I felt elated. With my top open, I stood as straight as I could in front of the imaging equipment. Buttons were pushed, and the technician asked me a ton of questions as a large sheet of clear plastic descended and smashed my breasts, one at a time. I stood still and tried my hardest to push my neck and head back out of the way of the machine as I watched the scanner hover above my pancaked breasts. *My neck can only go so far back anymore!* This was painful, but, hey, if you had experienced all that I had been through in this past year, you'd realize that "this ain't nothing but a thing". When my boob-squishing session finally ended, I walked back and sat in the small waiting room again before they called me to take my other test. Carol was still sitting there and she happily told me that she could connect four sets of multi-colored lights to decorate the front porch railing. I heard excitement and hope in her voice. *Thank you, Spirit, for using me and giving me the courage to help Carol heal.*

As she spoke, I looked at her, and you could have knocked me over with a dented ping pong ball. In amazement, I saw Carol's energy soften and a bright, beautiful smile shined in her eyes. A radiant glowing grass-green light beamed outward from her face, neck, arms, and hands. It was a saturated neon green light that was as brilliant as the color of new leaves in the springtime. When I focused more closely, I saw this luminous green energy extend beyond her outline as it lighted up the energy field around the outside of her body. Now her aura was glowing with this pure healing green, too. I felt the mighty presence of Archangel Raphael and all his/her angels with their outstretched hands sending wonderful green Reiki healing energy to Carol. Archangel Gabriel was there, too, with Gabby! I witnessed the entire waiting room filled with loving angels. Mesmerized, for about three minutes, I just sat there while I gazed at her sparkling green glow as if she were the Queen of the Emerald City. I visualized many heavily packed suitcases being thrown out of a doorway and knew that an energetic release of old, stale emotional baggage had taken place during this Divine time of spiritual healing for Carol.

"*NOW SHE HAS HOPE. SHE IS BEING HEALED...*

Wow! I took a deep breath. I realized the power of that unexpected mystical experience. Being blown away, I knew that I was filled with immense gratitude for meeting Carol and her daughter Gabby, and grateful for Spirit's healing energy that benefitted all of us. I immediately thanked Spirit for putting me where I needed to be this morning and for giving me strength and compassion... and the exact words to say.

As I began to slowly regain my composure, a technician wearing a buttoned-up white lab coat appeared and walked me to another imaging room for my ultrasound examination. This new room was so tiny and confining. *I'd lose my mind if I had to work in this closet! I bet this gal who performs ultrasound scans in this cramped space drives home every night talking to herself! This is crazy!* There was only room enough for a small steel exam table with a thin black leather cushion and the sterile white imaging equipment. The technician squeezed behind the scanner next to me as I did my best to get up onto the table, lie down, and turn to the right. *This is a monumental task for me, Lady!* It took me quite a while. Hot flames licked every nerve cell in my back. What was once so easy had now become a major challenge, but I didn't complain because I knew that it would take at least a year and a

Marc with a "C" - Hope from the Hereafter

half or more for my back to heal. Like an inchworm, I slowly wiggled myself into position. The technician was not very patient, but she had no choice if she wanted to get the test started. *I'm trying my best here, honey... just give me a minute. Maybe she should change her attitude!* LOL Finally, as I tenuously lay on my side on the table, she jellied me up with clear, icy cold goo, and began to take images as she pressed the scanner firmly into my left breast. I was freezing and aching so much that being back at home was all that I wanted. Tiredness and pain penetrated the muscles, tendons, and nerves in my entire back. *This boob stuff is so uncomfortable. Everything's uncomfortable anymore.* After about fifteen minutes, she had finished clicking her mouse on the imaging screen and told me to please stay on the table until she returned because she wanted the doctor to review my test results. She left me alone in the cold, dark, tiny room. The frigid jelly on my breast seemed to be hardening into a glob of roofing cement as I painfully lay on the steel table. My eyes looked up at the ceiling and I noticed the dimly-lit dated mauve wallpaper border which wrapped the room in thirteen inches of dingy mauve roses, circa 1972. *Oh, dear Lord! If I could, that border would be gone in a second. Whatever possessed someone to hang this wide funky-lookin' rose border in a room the size of a closet? What were they thinking? .... if they were thinking!* I laughed as I realized how critical I was being while I was stuck in this broom closet of a room. *Just relax, and think about those roses on that border. Roses are your beautiful psychic symbol for unconditional love. Chill.*

As I lay in the cold room lit only by the ultrasound screen, an overpowering force slowly entered the depths of my being. A feeling of immense love for Carol and Gabby softened my energy as it washed through me. My consciousness expanded and rocketed throughout the Universe. As total bliss encompassed me, I felt the depths of compassion and divine strength that I never knew I possessed. Experiencing a deep knowing of my life's purpose, I was astonished by this mystical spiritual awakening. My being almost exploded with the awesome encompassing love that had just occurred among me, Gabby, Marc, Carol, Spirit, and all the healing angels. Everything was right. I felt a deep inner peace that nothing could erase. I knew that I was here to bring light, love, and hope to others, which always returned to me doubled. *I truly belong here. I'm here because I am necessary.* Everything made perfect sense in my precious moment of profound clarity. I was connected to Divine Love and joy in a deep and sacred way, and I knew that all was well. *God, let me always bask in this bliss. Not a worry nor care could I have now. I know that I am part of Your Divine Plan, and it's all good.*

Throughout my entire life, there had constantly been two experiences that overwhelmingly moved me and brought my soul to tears... complete joy and profound sorrow. At this time, while I lay in that cramped ultrasound room, I was pulsating with a feeling of peace and joy that really and truly defied all understanding. Tears pooled in my eyes and trickled down my cheeks onto my short blue cotton top with the front ties. My entire being swelled with gratitude and love. *I am graced and overwhelmed by this blessing!* As I lay in amazement, I intuitively realized that my whole experience this morning had nothing at all to do with breast imaging and that my test results would be unremarkable, which as it turned out, they were. *I am here at this women's center on this cold and rainy day in December for one reason only, and it has absolutely nothing to do with boobs.* I thanked Spirit for putting me exactly where I was supposed to be and for all the good in my life.

As I blissfully lay on the table in the quiet of the dark, sterile room with the dated mauve roses, I heard my son Marc say to me, as clear as a bell and in the sweetest voice... **"Now, Mom, are you ready to write the book?"**

CHAPTER 2

GHOSTWRITER

Riding home from the Women's Center, I sat as quietly as a kid who was caught red-handed when he broke his mom's treasured vase that grandma had given her. There was nothing to say. Was I in shock? I felt exhilarated, but my exhausted mind felt as worn out as my body would have been after a ten-mile run. *Ha! A ten-mile run? You wish! More like a ten-foot shuffle right now!* Finally arriving home, we parked in the handicapped space and I turned and slid out of our car in the cold downpour, relying on my trusty cane to support me as I walked into our apartment. *We all need support in so many ways. Without this cane, I'd be out here on my behind! Without my family and friends, I don't know what would become of me.*

Feeling good to be home, I walked in the door and immediately headed for the kitchen. I grabbed a cup of Denny's delicious coffee from the pot and heated it in the microwave before I even took off my soaking wet coat. I swallowed a big gulp... *Mmmmm... Oh, this was truly worth the wait!* My drenched coat dripped water onto the wooden floor as I hung it over the hook on the door. I was spent and so grateful to be home again. Sitting at the dining table, I sipped my yummy decaf with almond milk and stared into the beveled mirror above the buffet. I felt Marc's energy all around me as I thought about what had just happened and what he wanted me to do.

The evening before, I had a conversation with Andie. She's an amazing psychic medium and one of my most treasured friends. She has the soothing and soft energy of Mother Mary who cradles you in her arms and soothes the day away. Her words brought me comfort and her laughter was contagious. *She is my favorite friend to laugh with!* She always knows the right words to say. And she's witty.... we're birds of a feather. Together, we could cause big trouble! Oh, do we have stories!? About ten minutes into our conversation, she got a vision. Andie told me that she "saw" many cars driving into the cemetery where Marc was interred. The cars were jam-packed with his friends and all kinds of people that he had helped in his life. She said that this was something huge… "an unending line of cars packed with people… a car caravan driving into the cemetery… they were driving past Marc's burial niche… so many people and friends… cars went on forever. Marc's here with me now…he says this is big." She tried to make clearer sense of this vision that came to her. "Are you getting anything?"

Andie and I had completely different psychic signs but we were always on the same page. We could usually connect the dots. As Andie shared her vision, I had an instant knowing. *This is about writing the book!* Andie had no clue that I was tossing around the idea of doing what Marc had asked me to do for him. Wondering how this was all linked together, I asked her, "Does this have anything to do with writing a book?"

There was a long pause. "Oh, my Lord… yes, oh yes! That's what this is all about. Oh, I just got goosebumps and chills!" She was quiet for a moment and then began speaking again, "Marc is pure healing energy. They're showing me his light! He lived on this earth as a Light Worker to help others. He knew what he was sent here to do and he did it. Yes, this *is* about a book… a book that will give hope and comfort to others. It's something big."

I sighed, knowing that Marc was prodding everybody on the entire planet to talk to me about writing this book. He wasn't letting up on me! *I get it! I get it! Wow, you're determined!* I was so grateful to my friend for the mini-reading she gave me. "Honey, thanks so much for sharing your vision with me. I have been getting the message to write a book about the signs that Marc sends to help me heal. Your vision was the validation I needed to hear. Yeah, I know what I need to do now. Thanks, and I love you."

"Yes, Ma'am, this book is important and you need to write it, and don't thank me — thank Marc." Andie had found a new friend! A couple of months after he had dropped his body, she met Marc for the first time when he came to her during a mediumship reading for me. Those two connected immediately. That reading was spot on, and Marc came through humorously loud and clear. Ever since then, Marc called her "Aunt Andie" and spent a lot of time with her. Being lighthearted, they grooved on each other's similar energies, and eventually, she became my special messenger from Marc. *That's hysterical... Marc's using a medium to give me his signs! Marc, you're too much!* Marc and I talked often, and I could hear him when he spoke, but I couldn't understand why he didn't give me some messages directly. Marc told Andie that there were a few important things that he couldn't tell me because there were times when he knew that I was still in a fragile condition, dealing with my sorrow, and it would be too painful for me to talk with him directly. Until I had healed a little bit more, Marc needed to come to someone who understood my fragile emotional state and could relay his messages to me with loving-kindness. He wanted a caring, compassionate, and gentle female friend to pass these profound messages from him along to me. Marc trusted Andie. Her heart was with me all the way, and with her soft and sweet love, Andie relayed whatever Marc wanted her to share with me. She was my Earth Angel. Writing this book was something he needed her to discuss with me. Andie would be the one to validate the idea of writing the book that I had been constantly thinking about but resisted. I didn't know the first thing about becoming a new writer. It was another episode of me not feeling good enough. I had to shake that thought faster than I could swat a hungry mosquito. *My mind can sometimes be a neighborhood that isn't safe to visit! There are places in my mind where I can't be... don't go there! Let that stuff go.*

During the last month or so, I had the "feeling" that I was supposed to write a book, and this weighed heavily on my mind. Boomeranging back to me, no matter how much I tried to shake the thought, the idea of a book kept popping up in my head. *Write a book. Write a book.* ***Write a book!*** *I know that if a thought is from my mind, it will come and it will go. I also know that if it's from Spirit, the "thought" will keep returning until I act on it. This is definitely from Spirit, and my team is persistent!*

Marc's signs and messages to me were important and they took a lot of energy from him. I knew that he had to lower his vibration and I had to raise mine for us to connect. That's a lot of work for a departed soul. I was so grateful for Marc's signs. Those signs made me feel as if his arms were wrapped around me, sending calm to my soul. My heart lifted with hope and my body relaxed with every comforting sign that he sent. I took notice and was on high alert for signs from Marc. I knew that I had to keep an eye open for them. Some signs were crazy, some were sweet, and some were downright unbelievable, and they were all priceless treasures to me. I needed them because I was enmeshed in the process of grieving. Reassuring me that he was fine, he sent these signs which became colorful rainbows of hope to me every day. I don't know if I could have gone on without them.

One night I had a lucid dream. As I slept, I felt that I was still awake in this dream and could manipulate this dream and change the outcome. I saw myself holding a book and I heard a man say to me, "This will touch all those who grieve and need hope." I had the feeling that the man who spoke to me was an angel. I looked closely at the book he handed me. It was the size and weight of a bible. There was no title on the deep orange leather cover and I was surprised to see my name inscribed in gold on the lower right-hand corner. This was my book! Then the dream ended and I knew that my future was urging me to embrace writing a book. No one had a clue that I had considered writing Marc's story, and not knowing where to begin, I was still teetering on the fence regarding this project. I was afraid, and that wasn't a good way to start. I asked

Marc for a special sign that would validate this book stuff once and for all.

Late one evening, while I was praying, I stopped to talk to Marc. Suddenly, I felt him there with me, so I asked him, "Honey, both you and Andie told me to write a book. Seriously? I'm seventy years old! Do you really want me to write a book about you?"

"Yes, and your age doesn't fit into this equation." Marc continued, *"The book is necessary and must be written."* Marc's tone was one of determination, and I knew that this was very important to him because those were not words that he would have spoken to me while he was here. They were more like words that you would hear Moses on a mountain top proclaiming to the crowd below or words the judge would say when he pounded his gavel and sentenced you to life in prison. Marc's tone was serious.

I asked, "Marc, are you sure about me writing a book? I've never written a book. Honey, it's gonna tell our entire story. Are you certain that you want me to do this?"

Marc responded, *"Yeah, Mom. So many people share my same story and so many parents share your same pain of losing a child. You witnessed that with Carol… you shared my signs and messages that brought you comfort, and you gave her proof that Gabby and her loved ones are always with her, even after death. What Spirit prompted you to do for Carol brought her hope, Ma. With this book, we are going to help so many people sort out their feelings, let go of grief, and heal their pain. Mom, we will give all of them hope. Please, for me, and Spirit… write the book."*

I was worried that I would be an unknown author and that, after all my hard work, the book would get lost in a sea of other tomes. Although I loved to write, I knew in my heart that many people would criticize me and judge both me and Marc after they read the book, and I didn't want to go through that. I had been through enough. Marc knew what I was thinking.

"Who cares what people think? Rejection is just the opinion of someone who thinks they got it all together. Mom, you know nobody on Earth has it all together! When they

point at you, and they will, that's on them. You were called to write this book and no other person can do this job. What you write will be very important. You are a Light Worker, Ma, and this is how you are being called to help others heal. Spirit and I will give you the words. It'll be fine. You can share love and hope. It's all good."

Although this would be the toughest story of my life for me to tell, I promised Marc that I would take on this daunting project just for him. I thought for a couple of minutes. *What the heck? What do I have to lose? With Spirit on my side, I can do this.* "Hey, Marc, do you promise that you and Spirit will help me? I'm sure you can sense my fear."

"*Of course!*" Those were the words he used whenever anyone ever asked him for his help and hearing them melted my heart. His reassurance was all I needed. "*Thanks, Ma. And remember, this is your book and you are the author. I am only your ghostwriter — get it? BOO!*"

Oh, Geez!!! *Are you kidding me? You're too much!* Marc was playing with me... he loved to tease me... and I swear I saw him wink at me. I laughed out loud hearing his "ghostwriter" statement. *Marc is a ghost helping me write this book!!! That's crazy!!! Bahaha!* "Hey, Marc, you gotta add "Ghostwriter" to your resume!" His teasing brightened my energy and I knew that he was happy because I was happy. Marc was now my writing partner... my GHOSTwriter! It seemed so absurd. *This is crazy! But, at least Marc's going to help me.* I felt some of the tension leave my body and I started to relax as I laughed. Then, all of a sudden, a heavy thought crossed my mind and my muscles tightened... *Where do I start?* "Marc, please tell me where I should begin. I'm gonna need a ton of help."

"*Introduce me first, Mom. Then tell our readers about you. I'll tell you what you need to write. You're gonna do a great job, Ma. If we bring hope to even one soul on earth, it'll be well worth the effort. Thank you, Mom. I know how tough this will be for you, but I also know that writing will help you to heal. I love you and I'll be guiding you the entire time. You'll know what to write. I promise you will."*

About a week later, my sweet niece, who had no idea about my book project, brought me a beautiful and unique gift for my upcoming birthday. As she walked through the door she handed me a gorgeous gift bag and said, "Happy Birthday... this is from Marc." I truly believed that Marc led her to buy whatever gift was concealed in the lovely bag, and I was very grateful. As I opened the bag, I told her that I was so appreciative to get a gift from Marc and that it was so sweet of her. I reached into the bag and removed my fragile, beautifully wrapped birthday present. I peeled back the tissue paper that caressed my gift, and a gorgeous antiqued white rose revealed its presence to me. I heard my breath leave me. *Oh, how delicate and beautiful!* Roses are my psychic sign for unconditional love, and immediately, I felt Marc's love wrapped around me just as if he were holding me in his strong arms. My eyes teared up as I gazed at this amazing flower that I held in my hand and knew that Marc had sent it to me.

Marc spoke to me, *"Look closer, Mom. I picked this gift, especially for you. Happy Birthday. I love you."* I could see his bright smile. I took a closer look at this meaningful gift. Unbelievably, the petals of that fragile rose were delicately crafted from the pages of a book! *The pages of a book!!?? You've got to be kidding me!* I got chills up and down my body. And, incredibly, a small bright orange cut-out butterfly looked as if it had just flown in and landed on one of the rose petals. *An orange butterfly??!!* Orange was Marc's favorite color and his entire world was orange! I got goosebumps! I had just received the clearest validation from Marc telling me to write the book! He had just sent me two of the most awesome gifts ever...a birthday rose with his unconditional love and the courage to write our book of hope.

"Thanks for the birthday present, Marc. You're so sweet, and I love you. Okay, honey, as difficult as it will be for me, I'll write the book for you. Together we'll give others hope."

It was official! Marc and I had just set off on an incredible soul journey together, and it didn't matter at all that we were separated by space and time.

An orange butterfly on
a rose with words.

PART TWO:

JOURNEY ON

Joy Elaine Reed

CHAPTER 3

BUTTERFLIES IN A YELLOW ROOM

It was Labor Day weekend. *How appropriate that my baby chose this time to be born! This is a weekend that I'll never forget!* Marc had been born forty-six years earlier, two days after I went to the hospital to deliver. He was in no great hurry to come to Earth. *This baby must be super-comfy in there because it's takin' a good old time. I might as well make a permanent move into this hospital.* After two days of panting and pushing, the doctor finally announced, "It's a boy!" *Oh, Lord, I'm so excited... I feel as if I've done something tremendous! I feel as if I have won the Academy Award for best actress or something! I am so proud! He's finally here!* My newborn baby boy was long and tall and weighed three pounds more than a five-pound bag of potatoes. He looked just like his dad without the eyeglasses, and we named him Marc Alan. He was eight pounds and three ounces of pure baby love. The first time that I looked into his bright blue eyes, I was hooked. Marc was my firstborn son, and he had the distinction of being the first newborn that I had ever held. I was simply in awe as I counted his tiny fingers and toes. *What a perfect tiny creature. And he's ours!* This was all new to me, and I was as thrilled as I was petrified. I knew that I was in no way, shape, or form ready to be Marc's mother or anybody else's mother. *I can't even take care of myself, let alone this tiny baby!* I was amazed by how only one moment in time, one blink of an eye, changed my life so profoundly. *Oh, Lord, I'm somebody's mother! This precious baby has altered my entire identity. Yesterday, I was me, and today I am Marc's mother. Life is so awesome, although I'm not so sure that I am cut out to be a "Mom". I guess it's too late to think about that now!*

What do I do with this baby? Why do mother giraffes know what to do with their babies, and I don't have a clue? I was filled with fear. I had never even considered "Motherhood". *We make plans and God laughs.* Thankfully, love conquered my fears as my heart grew bigger in deep devotion for this tiny guy that I held in my arms. Even though I was a maternal newbie, my instinct to love and protect my baby kicked in immediately. I felt that Marc was okay with me being a rookie mom. He didn't judge my lack of baby smarts. I had a strange feeling that before he was even born, Marc picked me especially to be his mother.

In those days, there was no gender-reveal celebration. You found out the sex of your baby after the doctor took that quick first look! And God forbid, you didn't mess with the "baby- colors"! In 1975, blue was only appropriate for a boy and pink was only appropriate for a girl. Period. You didn't dare interchange them or mix up these hues. *What will happen if I paint my daughter's or son's bedroom blue, purple, or avocado? Why are there all kinds of crazy "baby rules" that have been handed down from the beginning of time? It's way too much for me. I'm a rule breaker.* With our newborn in my arms, we left the hospital and took Marc home to his bedroom painted a "safe" buttercup yellow with colorful butterfly decals on the walls, and particle-board cartoon animals hanging on the wall above the bassinet where we did all Marc's diaper changing. *This room's very gender friendly. Honestly, I wish that we had painted it bright purple!*

I was so grateful when my mom and dad came over to our little cape cod cottage every day to help with Marc's care and teach me the nuances of newborns. Unfortunately, our lives soon changed as we packed to leave our cottage because our landlord decided to sell his house and move into ours. And, he told us the news on the day Marc was born! *Seriously? Nice timing! We have a new baby here to consider! I'm in no condition to move. Who does this? So not cool at all. Some people need to be shaken, not stirred!*

Mom and Dad insisted that it was no problem for all of us to move in with them (again), and so we left our cozy cottage with the painted yellow bedroom with butterflies and moved into my parent's house and the master bedroom they had fixed for us. Marc's dad and I were both school teachers and he worked two jobs, so he missed spending a lot of time with us. Fortunately, Gram and Pap were always there to help and support us. *Thank God!* I had no clue what do to with a baby. *I feel so useless as a mother.* My mom showed me how to swaddle Marc in a blanket to help him feel safe and protected. I also learned how to test the temperature of his formula by putting a few drops from the bottle on the inside of my elbow. I learned how to launder cloth diapers, as disposable diapers were expensive and only to be used for special occasions. *More "baby rules"*. Feeding, dressing, cleaning, and diapering had to be taught to me. *Thanks to my parents I'm finally getting my "Mommy Train" on the right track.*

From the start, Marc's life became a challenge for us all. He had problems taking his bottle, and whenever he took a sip of formula, he would ball up his little knees in pain. It was awful that he couldn't eat... all he could do was scream! *Marc, what can I do to help you? Come on, honey, just try to eat.* Gram tried every trick she knew, but nothing seemed to help settle Marc down to be able to drink a bottle. We took him to the pediatrician who diagnosed his condition as "colic" and prescribed a barbiturate to calm Marc enough so that he could eat without becoming distressed. *Maybe Marc can feel my fear about taking care of him?* It was so unfortunate that Marc's colic scared me as much as a hornet buzzing around the inside of my car while I was driving on the freeway. Constantly on edge, I was afraid that he would die if I couldn't get him to eat. *Anxietyville ain't a pretty place to visit.* Since we had tried everything and nothing had worked, I had no choice but to measure tiny drops of this barbiturate into my baby's mouth before giving him his formula. It calmed him down and allowed him to finally drink his bottle, but it was so sad that he could only do so if I medicated him. I loved him so and my muscles tightened every time I gave those drops to him. Poor Marc started on a rocky journey with constant challenges, and that was only the beginning.

People had told me that becoming a mother changes your life. The sleepless nights with three o'clock feedings, changing and washing all those cloth diapers, calling the pediatrician almost every day, and packing a diaper bag instead of a purse were, indeed, huge changes. My "time-to-grow-up metamorphosis" came by the way of a tiny baby and I realized that it was the moment for me to wave goodbye to my selfish world of ego. Now I cared about my baby more than I cared about myself, and that was a first. Motherhood grounded me, and I needed that. I felt good being Marc's mother. *I know that all things happen for a reason when the time is right.*

I adored Baby Marc. And, in my own life growing up, I felt deeply loved and adored. Although throughout my life, sometimes the love that I received from others came with conditions. As if I were a marionette - strings were attached. I had to behave and act in a certain manner. I had to be perfect. I had to excel. *Where did all those straight A's get me?* I had to go to school and behave, go to church and sit silently while wearing my white gloves, and take piano lessons and practice every day when sometimes I didn't want to do these things. I could never finish in second place. Even when I did everything right, it often did not seem good enough. *Is it this way for all of us? If I talk to a million people, would it be the same as this for them? Is this what love is all about? Do we all not feel good enough?* When I was on top of my game and followed all the rules, life was grand. When I was a little bit off the mark (and there were many times when I made big mistakes), life could turn crappy. Mostly I got major loving, but sometimes I got the "silent treatment" mixed in. I hated the "silent treatment". Later, I would learn that I can't make other people happy. I am who I am and I did my best. I never in my entire life wanted to hurt anybody. I was never going to please everyone, anyway. *It's impossible to please others. They have to be happy on their own. People have to choose happiness. I have to give up people-pleasing and trying to make other people happy because it's a waste of my energy. I know it's a tall order, but I just gotta love myself and let others figure out happiness for themselves.*

Most of us have probably been loved but have had conditions for love and acceptance put upon us. That was usually the way it went. When we did well, we got hugs. When we didn't act or behave like our parents/relatives/teachers/cops/bosses, etc. wanted us to, who knew what repercussions would be in store for us? I realized that most of the love we got in life was usually conditional and based on parental expectations. All loving parents have expectations... otherwise, they wouldn't be loving parents. I dearly appreciated my loving parents. Perhaps, unfortunately, our mothers and fathers raised us in the same way that they were raised, which may or may not have been for the best. We shouldn't judge them for that, because that's all they knew. They did the best they could with what they had. *We're writing and reading this book now, right? So we must give our parents a mental high five and credit for doing a good job of raising us. We must thank them and forgive them if necessary. We all do the best we can when it comes to love. They did, and we did, and we learned love lessons on the way.*

Most beautifully, in my life, Marc put no conditions on the love he gave to me. Being Marc's mother brought me the glorious, expansive feeling of unconditional love. He didn't care if I wasn't skilled in diapering him or if I sounded froggy when I sang lullabies to him. *This little guy puts up with a lot and still loves me.* He loved me totally with all his dear heart. He could care less that I was a clueless new mom. Marc's love for me was perfect and with no strings attached. I learned to love him back the same way. *Amazingly, a little tiny baby is teaching me the real meaning of love. Babies do that, you know. Thanks, Marc. I will be forever grateful for your unconditional love. Thank you, God, for this beautiful gift of new life. I am so glad to be Marc's mother. I promise that I'll do the best I can to love my new little one.*

CHAPTER 4

TOUCHY-FEELY

As a toddler, Marc was a lovable imp, and just looking at him made us grin. He was a mover and a groover and knew how to keep me on high alert. *I have to keep my eyes on him 24/7! Thank God that he's a good sleeper!* He was so inquisitive, and as he planned his next move, you could see the gears in his brain spinning and whirling. He was always up to something, but we were never sure what that something was until it happened. *Surprise!*

"See It - Touch It" was his motto. Nothing deterred Marc. Being extremely intelligent, he was determined to find out how things worked. To Marc, "Don't touch" meant "Touch it twice"! "No" was a word that held no weight. He knew what it meant, but he didn't care. *What I need is a wireless doggy fence with a short radius!!! At least I would know where Marc is most of the time!*

Marc was a quick study and spoke sophisticatedly before he was nine months old. As a sponge whose radar was attuned to every word ever spoken, I had to be very careful about any comments I made. *Watch your mouth around Marc...he loves new words! And he uses them, too!* He filed new words away in the vocabulary drawer of his mind and would use them correctly in the future, much to my dismay. You never knew what would come out of his mouth! His dynamic brain was always at work and verbalization was his strength. *I swear Marc could have been a two-year-old trial attorney... and would never lose a case!*

Marc couldn't bear feeling the tags or the seams in his clothing. He was super sensitive to feeling the clothes on his body and especially the pajamas that he wore all night. Those seams drove him so crazy he acted as if he were being burned with a branding iron. Marc was so bothered by the tactile stimulation of all those tags and seams that he tore the tags out of everything he ever wore. There were holes in the back of the neck of every jersey that he ever wore! At night he wore his pajamas inside out because the seams bothered him so. Growing up, he was also very sensitive to foods, lights, soaps, and you name it. *I swear, sometimes I think that he's an alien. Marc's so different. I just can't understand how things feel to him. I wish I were in his skin to see what this is all about!*

Because of his sensitivities, Marc learned to run before he could walk. At eleven months of age, Marc was talking up a storm but wasn't walking yet. I guessed that he was in no great hurry to get anywhere. One sunny afternoon, he was barefooted, and I put him out in the middle of Gram's front yard to play with his toys. The grass under his feet must have driven him crazy because he ran from the yard screaming and crying. I never anticipated his distress, but I was glad he was finally walking. *Who knew that the challenge of motherhood could be such a stormy mix of frustration and joy?*

Although his many sensitivities sometimes taxed my patience, Marc was my love bug from day one. I loved him with all my heart and soul, and he loved me back unconditionally. He loved *everyone* unconditionally. Marc had a heart as big as Texas and had more than enough love to fill the entire Universe. He was a bright sphere of love energy who came to me as a son, and I was grateful. Although mischievous, he was a sweet kid. He had love in his eyes. To know Marc was to adore Marc, he was that loving and special. He gave me more hugs and kisses than the stars in the sky. I can still picture him running to me with his arms flung open, ready to hug me as tightly as he could. *Toddlers' hugs are the best!* He was a blond, blue-eyed charmer, and twisted everyone who loved him around his little finger.

Thinking back, I would call Marc's energy fun, bright, soft, loving, impulsive, and excitedly over-the-top. He was intelligent, tender, peace-loving, and sensitive. He delighted in making everybody feel good and he had a quirky, keen sense of humor. Interacting with adults and being around animals were his favorite things. Marc was wooed by Mother Nature and would stay outside and play all day long. Marc found things he liked to do on his own. I think that Pap and I were the only two people in the world who ever appreciated what made Marc tick. I know Marc was grateful to have felt our understanding and unconditional love and was comforted by the deep spiritual bond that we all shared. Marc needed that connection and assurance desperately.

Marc always shined his bright light on others and taught me to be patient with him because he was trying to be the best he could be. I had heard that, by the age of three, people have formed all they need to know about how life works. Marc got that knowledge very early...he understood life with the wisdom of a ninety-three-year-old. I didn't get it yet. Marc taught me that I had a lot to learn. *Marc knows more than I do, and he's only three years old. Where the heck was I when the boat left the dock?*

Marc came into the world as a "sensitive intuitive". At that time, most of us didn't know anything about what was beyond our bodies. We only knew what we could see. We walked around thinking that our bodies were only made of flesh and blood. That's our physical bodies, but there's so much more. Who knew we all had energy bodies as well? Marc was born sensitive to all the energies around him. He was born an Empath, and I found out much later that I was one also. Empaths can feel the feelings of others. People, places, animals... Marc felt every bit of hate, anger, joy, frustration, love, grief, shame, and fear in the energies that surrounded him. That overload of emotions was tough on him. *That's tough on anybody! Empaths need to learn to ground and protect their energy. Too bad we don't come into this world with instructions tied to our wrists.* Who knew? As a toddler, Marc reacted to this energy immediately, and sometimes his behavior didn't make sense to us. It's a small wonder why he suffered from colic. No one in our family knew how to deal with a sensitive child. Nobody at this time knew or even thought that children could be born with intuitive sensitivities. *I can't imagine the difficult time Marc had living in his own body... negating his feelings because he took on all the feelings of others around him. I wish I had known about this when Marc was young.* But knowing about this would not have mattered because that was not how this hand was meant to be played out.

CHAPTER 5

BROTHERLY LOVE

My second love bug, Adam, came along five years after Marc was born, and he stole my heart. At ten pounds, ten ounces, he was my hefty little sumo wrestler and I adored him. I swear that he looked big enough to walk out of the hospital on his own!! He instantly became my priceless treasure. *What a dear child you are, Baby Adam. Thanks for choosing me to be your Mother. I love you, big guy!*

Although it was incredibly painful, being in labor with a heavier-than-ten-pounder didn't matter to me because I had just given birth to a new somebody to love. But I admit that it was a wild trip. *Why would you ever think to have "natural childbirth"? Are you crazy? Without a pain pill, you just pushed a two-year-old out of your body! Is there anyone here who wants to meet a strong woman? Here I am, and don't get in my way now.* That I had just birthed an almost eleven-pound bag of potatoes made me realize that I could do anything! Adam made me strong! *Unlike my pelvic floor!*

Adam completed our family. I had never thought that after I had married, I would raise two sons. I have loved children all my life. Having one big boy and one little boy was a good feeling for me. While I held baby Adam in my arms, Marc became hyper-attentive and took care of all my needs. Of course, he wanted to reaffirm and ensure my love for him, too.

Like Marc, Adam was a loving soul... he was such a sweetie. There was a five-year age gap between the boys which made their differences obvious. Adam was husky, contemplative, and calm. Marc was slim, impulsive, and excitable. Although they were intellectuals, they processed information differently. Adam was the thinker, Marc was the doer. From a young age, Adam seemed to know who he was, and Marc seemed to be searching. They loved each other deeply. What brought them together as brothers were their kind hearts and their love of life. They were wonderful packages of kindness and caring wrapped in ribbons of fun. *I adore my sons and know how blessed I am. It feels so right to have them in my life. I have so much fun with them. I love little kids... and these special little kids are ours!* Both Marc and Adam were connected to me and each other with a thick golden cord of love that grew stronger every day.

Parenting these boys was a real trip, sometimes smooth and sometimes rocky, but I wouldn't have had it any other way. Although the discipline of children has been a challenge for parents throughout the ages, my nonexistent "Mother's Book" came in handy if and when the boys questioned my parental authority...and I remember one particular time when Adam was about four years old...

"Adam, you have to go to bed now. Let's Go."

"No, I don't wanna. I'm staying up late today." Adam liked to push the limits.

"No, honey, it's time for bed."

Then Adam turned to me and asked, "Ma, don't you think I'm a big kid?"

"Yes, I do."

"Then let me stay up later...please?" Adam liked to plead.

I watched Adam as he lightly ran his index finger between his nose and upper lip. He always did that when he was tired. (That started as a baby when he would suck his thumb and use his pointer finger to rub the edge of his blanket along his upper lip to put himself to sleep. Without his blanket, Adam would fret when he needed to nap and rest. His plain old thumb wouldn't do the trick... he also had to hold a blanket to his lip. *We gotta go through his whole production when every other kid in the entire world just needs a pacifier!* One afternoon, during his usual nap time, baby Adam was fussing and crying as we drove home from the mall. Unfortunately, his blanket wasn't with us. *Oh, oh, we're in deep trouble now!* We quickly searched the car for tissues, a rag, a towel, a receipt, or anything! As Adam continued to cry, we found nothing that would work like his blanket. *I'm half tempted to take off my blouse and let him use that if it will calm him down.* We were stumped so we gave him his teddy bear to hold and hoped that Teddy would comfort him. He began plucking the fur from his teddy bear's head. Then he rolled it into a little furry ball between his thumb and index finger and slid it back and forth across his upper lip while he sucked his thumb and fell asleep. *Really? Who does that?* Resourceful Adam's unique technique was the disappearing act for the fur on Teddy's head, ears, hands, and feet while Adam plucked his way to sleepy-time. Teddy became as bald as a Mexican hairless puppy. As a brother would do to be helpful, Marc would always alert us when Adam was tired by telling us, "Adam's pluckin' again!". *Oh, dear! Are we having fun yet? Poor Teddy's the victim of pluckin' and suckin'!)*

    I continued to get Adam to go to sleep. "Come on, honey, it's time for bed."

    Adam shook his head. "No, it's not."

    I held up my pointer finger and said, "Wait, I'll be right back." I rose out of my chair and walked into my bedroom. Since I was near my bathroom, it was perfect timing for a toilet break. Adam wouldn't be the wiser. A few minutes later, I returned to the living room, where Adam sat in front of the television.

    "You have to go to sleep now, Adam. It's bedtime."

    "Why?" Both Marc and Adam liked to ask questions.

    "Because I just checked my "Mother's Book" and it says on page sixty-three that when you're four years old, you have to go to bed by seven o'clock."

"Is it seven o'clock now?" I nodded yes. Adam thought a moment and replied, "Oh...Okay." Case closed. To sleep he went. Easy-peasy.

Adam didn't question my "Mother's Book" until he was about eight years old. That's the same time when the Easter Bunny, Tooth Fairy, and Santa became suspects, too. One time Adam was fooling around and being naughty, and I told him, "In my Mother's Book on page ...yadda, yadda." He came right up to me, put the palms of his hand up, looked me in the eyes, and demanded, "I wanna see this book." *Oh, no! Say it isn't so!!* The words he uttered were the death decree for my omnipotent tome of motherhood. Adam killed my "Mother's Book" with one sentence. My strategy was now kaput. *Thank God that it worked like a dream for so many years. I guess that's the end of that!* Amazingly, I rarely had to open the Mother's Book for Marc! It seemed like Adam was our rebel, but who knew?

While we left every day to teach school, Gram and Pap provided personal daycare for our sons. Although raising kids for the second time challenged my aging parents, my Mom and Dad were thrilled to help us. Even though Adam and Marc tired them out, I think they were happy to have the boys around because they loved kids, and I was their only child. I was adopted and I knew that Dad and Mom would have loved to have had more children. Unfortunately, that couldn't happen.

Grandparents are priceless gems. They are wise and teach so many lessons to me and my children. Gratitude was what I learned from my patient parents. I was grateful for their love and support without charge. We could never repay them for all they did for us. *We all need to be grateful for the love and compassion of others. We should put ourselves in their shoes and appreciate their time, effort, and concern for our welfare. Kindness is an act of mercy and love, and we must always appreciate it.*

There are many times in our lives when we will need assistance from others. If we need help, we must ask for help. This rule applies to asking the angels and also asking the people in our lives. Asking for help when we need it doesn't make us weak, by any means. On the contrary, it means that we are strong enough to realize and accept that we are needy in some way. And, trust me, everyone will be needy at some point in their lives. Although most people will see our difficulty and come to our aid, there will be times when it may become necessary to ask for help. Remember, most people don't know what you need unless you tell them. It's a blessing for both the giver and receiver when you let go of control and allow others to take charge. My aging parents generously offered their help to us and they were a godsend. I knew that with our sons in their lives, situations were difficult for my parents because my boys were a handful. But I'm sure that they were used to it because, when I was growing up I was two and a half handfuls all on my own!

To give Gram a nap break, every day Pap walked to the neighborhood car dealership a couple of blocks away with either Marc (before Adam was born), or Adam (while Marc was in school). Dad enjoyed talking with his friends and our next-door neighbor who worked there. In reality, Dad went to the car dealership to get the lineup for the upcoming weekend horse races, and to find out what time the guys would be leaving for the track on Saturday. Dad was a great guy with no other vices than the ponies. He didn't smoke or drink, so going to the horse races was what Dad lived for every week! Amazingly enough, Dad never lost when he placed a bet on a horse! Never!? When he came home from the races and Mom asked how he did, Dad always told her… "I won thirty-five dollars". Every single week, he won thirty-five dollars at the races…not ten dollars or fifty dollars or eighty-eight dollars or a million dollars…always thirty-five bucks. And, it was apparent that Dad never lost money either. *Dad, really? Every single week?* Mom never said a word, although she knew what was going on. Mom wasn't stupid - she was as sly as a fox. She needed her afternoon nap breaks, and I guessed that she figured that they were surely worth "thirty-five dollars" a week to her.

In the meantime, while Pap was at the garage talking horses with his friends, one of my sweet little angels was on the loose and thrilled to be ignored. Having the time of his life because I wasn't with him to keep him in line, Marc or Adam (or sometimes both!) climbed into every car in the showroom and bounced around, adjusted the steering wheels and seats, and pushed every single button. Turning the steering wheel to make the tires squeak on the floor was a particular rush for Marc or Adam. They tested all the horns to see which ones they liked the best. Marc was the experienced button pusher and you would know wherever he was because the trunks and glove compartments would all pop open. Dad was checking the race lineup and was oblivious to my excited little guys. *Why take them to expensive theme parks when they can just come to the new car showroom? I bet these salesmen cringe whenever Marc and Adam climb into the new red sports car while Dad is sitting with the guys and picking a horse in the second race! Oh, my Lord, I can see the look on the salesmen's faces now!* Hey, the salesmen's hands were kinda tied and their mouths were tightly zipped since every car my dad had ever bought came from their car dealership! *Some things are best left unsaid!*

Pap and Gram were beyond generous and extremely giving of their time, money, and love. They spared nothing when it came to Adam and Marc and traveled way beyond the realm of generosity. I was grateful for all the help that I got and I knew that we were blessed. God sent his blessings to me with sweet little boys and awesome parents. *It's all good.*

Adam and Marc

Joy Elaine Reed

CHAPTER 6

THE REAL WINNER

As a young schoolboy, Marc's life became as dark as spilled ink in a cave with no candlelight. He was talented intellectually and school was almost meaningless to him. Bored and antsy, once he finished his seat work he probably couldn't sit still, so I'm sure he was like me, and he invented things to do. Unfortunately, intellectual maturity and "antsiness" did not seem to be tolerated by the nuns who were the teachers at his school. His teachers seemed hesitant to want to deal with a student who didn't fit into their cookie-cutter mold. Marc must have frustrated them, and in turn, this private school became like a torture chamber from which he couldn't escape.

He was bullied unmercifully by some boys in his class. Because he didn't fit in with the boys, he played with the girls who accepted him. This caused more bullying and hateful remarks. Boys called him "Gay", and made his life a living hell. The teachers got on his case for playing with the girls. Poor little Marc left his comfortable, loving, and safe home every weekday and then went to school to be bullied and reprimanded. *He's gettin' it from both sides, isn't he?* Oh, how my heart ached for him. *The most important feeling a child can feel is that he is safe. Marc feels so vulnerable. He's scared to death!* In the 1980s there was no "bullying awareness". I met with his teachers and asked if Marc started anything, fought, or called anybody names, or if he was responsible for the bullying incidents in any way. He was not. His teachers and I discussed options to stop the bullying, but not a blessed thing seemed to have been done to help Marc. None of the other boys in his class were punished for their mean behavior. The bullying continued. Believe it or not, I was told that Marc was the problem! If Marc had done something wrong or fought with other kids or disobeyed, you'd better believe he would have been reprimanded because children all need to know right from wrong. But, in this case, Marc was not the perp, Marc was the victim! I was so angry...*Marc is not the problem. Hate is the problem. Ignorance is the problem. Stupidity and heartlessness are the problems. Wake up, people! Nobody has the right to hurt another human being... ever!*

  I felt the pain and frustration of my grade school son being victimized. *Shooting me dead wouldn't hurt me as much as my heart aches right now.* Home-schooling and cyber schools were non-existent at that time. I complained to Marc's teachers and principal but nobody heard me nor wanted to hear me. Nobody stopped what was going on. *What could a seven-year-old do to make haters hate so fiercely? Where's the compassion?* Fear and pain gripped Marc every day of his life. I felt his pain, too. We both felt as if we were stranded on a deserted island with no one to rescue us. At his school, Marc had no friends his age, nor teachers who seemed to understand him. In our family, attending parochial school was a mandate and nobody could upset the apple cart by attending public school. At that time, I always respected my elders and everyone in authority, and I was taught not to question nor contradict them, which left us with no options. *I'm a fearful little girl raising a kid. Not working out too good, is it?* At that time I was unaware that I had my voice and that I could set boundaries. In my family, I always did what I was told.

  When Marc was in the second grade, he fell off his bike and gashed his head as he flew over the handlebars into the street. He needed stitches, so I took him to the emergency room. The doctor sewed him back together, good as new. He had a concussion. As the doctor checked his eyes and ears, he pulled three small pea size gray rocks from his right ear canal. *What?* The doctor asked Marc how the stones got in his ear. Marc said he didn't know. All I could see in my mind were the bullies that beat him up on the playground, knocked him to the ground, and pushed his head into the dirt. *How else would stones get into his ear?* My heart ached for this sweet young boy with no friends who was only trying to make it to the three o'clock bell. *Dear God, Please help my baby.* I spent so many nights crying myself to sleep with the pain of hate and ignorance stabbing into my chest. *He's just a little kid! How can a six-year-old make a teacher feel threatened? Marc's a loving little boy!*

Marc began having asthma attacks when he was about seven years old. He would wake up in the middle of the night unable to breathe. I would immediately take him to the bathroom and run the hot water in the shower until the bathroom became like a sauna. I took him to see our family doctor who prescribed an inhaler and told me it was much easier to take him outside to sit in the night air whenever he couldn't catch his breath during an asthma attack. I continued to use the bathroom/sauna because it worked for us. *It's so scary when my son can't breathe. I'll do whatever I can to help him catch his breath. It'll be all right.*

I remembered the time that Marc brought his report card home when he was in the sixth grade and he earned a D in Reading. *What? Reading? Can't you read? This must be a crazy mistake!* Earning A's on all his Reading worksheets, I knew there was a problem. When I went to see his teacher, she told me that Marc tested at the college level on the recent Reading placement test. *Okay....* Then that nun told me that since he tested on the college level and was only reading at a sixth-grade level, she gave him a D because he wasn't reading up to his potential. *What!!!!! You've got to be kidding me! I can't believe what I am hearing! Just shoot me now! He gets straight A's on all his worksheets. He is in the sixth grade, you know. That's the grade you teach...grade six!* This teacher never gave him college material to read. He read his sixth-grade books just like all the other kids in class, and they didn't all get D's in reading. Marc had been singled out. Marc's reading wasn't "good enough" for his teacher. I spoke with the principal. I told her that I didn't care that Marc got a D on his report card. *Who the heck gives a damn what reading grade is written on your sixth-grade report card? I just care if my son can read. Why is Marc being singled out?* I was concerned because of the ludicrousness of this situation... Marc earned all A's in reading and got a D on his report card, which he did not earn. Why would his teacher do this? The nun who was the school principal said that she would "look into the matter". *Here we go again. Fat chance of this ever happening. I'm ready to burn this school down to the ground.* Unfortunately, Marc lived his whole life feeling that he wasn't "good enough". Watching this loving child be so hurt brought me to tears. *This is not how life is supposed to be lived. There's too much pain!*

Both Marc and I lived in that box labeled "Not Good Enough". Long ago I had self-worth issues and didn't realize that I deserved respect. It took me a long time until I realized that we must all learn to love and respect ourselves to gain the love and respect of others. We needed to set boundaries about what we would allow and what we would not accept. *Setting boundaries is scary at first, especially when we're young and we're taught that we don't have a voice. We don't want to rock the boat or hurt others, but by not setting boundaries we are hurting ourselves. Once our boundaries are set, the kinks come out of the chain and everything seems to smooth out.* Unfortunately, it took me ages to muster the courage to set personal boundaries. I kept allowing others to hurt me. I was afraid to open my mouth when it needed to be opened. I was afraid to contradict any person in authority. I was unaware that I could stand up for myself and be heard. Being unable to set boundaries for myself meant that I couldn't help Marc set boundaries for himself. *At the time I didn't know how to help Marc be whom he needed to be.*

There was an event that I remembered when Marc was about eight years old. That's when he swam for a local swim team.

Marc's body was engineered to swim, and in the water, Marc was a slick fish who could move faster than any hungry great white shark looking for a quick dinner. Gold medals and trophies filled the entire top of his dresser in his bedroom, and first-place finishes became a habit for him. He had qualified for an invitational swim meet that was almost a four-hour drive from our home, and he wanted to swim in two events. *Hmmm. Should we spend all day with a million screaming kids just to watch you jump in the water twice?* Marc's dad and I pondered if we wanted to get up before the crack of dawn to sit for eleven or more hours watching kids swim back and forth as if they were competing in an aquatic tennis match. We were both hesitant, but Marc wanted to swim in this meet because there were a lot of kids from many different school districts and he loved to meet new people. So, on that Saturday we drove for what seemed to be a long week of days, to a remote town nestled in the mountains. The packed parking lot was our tipoff that this event was a big deal and that other parents were as crazy as we were. We walked into the pool area which reverberated with the deafening sound of hundreds of excited kids, then we gave Marc a good luck hug, and found seats in the stands where all the other parents and siblings were seated. *I brought lunches, I brought snacks, I brought books, and I brought Adam, but oh, how I wish that I had brought my earplugs!* We knew that we wouldn't see Marc again until later in the day when he had finished competing in both events. *This is going to be one of those long days of waiting.*

    In the late morning, Marc won a gold medal for finishing in first place in breaststroke for his age group. *Yay! He did it again. This kid's a swimmer, for sure!* In the middle of the afternoon, just when we were ready to take a much-needed nap, Marc was poised at the starting block again, waiting for the starter to fire his starting pistol. BANG! In near-choreographed unison, eight boys dived into the water and free-styled their compact bodies back and forth across the pool four times. As we watched and cheered, we saw that Marc raised his head out of the water to take a breath with every single stroke. *Hey…What's he doing? I've never seen him swim like this before. I can't believe my eyes!* We watched him swim each lap and fall further behind all the other boys. Of course, guess who finished last? I expected to see tears and a hanging head as Marc walked into the locker room, but he did not look upset. He changed his clothes and we met him down by the pool, ready to make the trek home. His father and I were disturbed because we had driven halfway across the globe in the dark to get here, and spent the entire day inhaling chlorine to watch Marc swim as if he were just learning the strokes. I was also tired, upset, and confused. *I'll talk to him.* I asked Marc why he swam freestyle and came up for a breath after each stroke. "That's not how you swim freestyle. What happened?"

Marc looked at me and was silent. I waited for an answer. Then he said, "Did you see that kid on the block next to me, Ma? He had on a red swimsuit and he's a little bit shorter than me. He's as old as me, and he has a sister named Jessica. He's from Kensington Valley which is almost in the middle of the state. I met him here this morning and he was so nice to me, and we spent the whole day together. He's so funny and he made me laugh. We had a lot of fun together all day. He's my new friend, Mom...I just couldn't beat my friend. I wanted him to win."

Oh my Lord! Marc had finally felt the beauty of acceptance and friendship for the first time in his life, and he would do nothing to spoil that experience. He just wanted his friend to win that race. *Talk about kindness and caring!* How could I be upset with Marc? *That's always been the loving way Marc treats everyone. He wants more for others than he wants for himself. There's no greater blessing on earth than to be a friend and have a friend.* On the outside and deep inside, my heart was smiling because Marc had, for a brief time, ultimately found what he so desperately desired. *I am so happy for him! He found a friend!* Kind-hearted Marc turned out to be the real winner for the day!

CHAPTER 7

DARKENED ROOMS AND RAINBOWS

I hate it when I hear, "Mom, I have a headache." Oh, not again! Marc's migraines started when he was in the first grade. At least twice during the week the school nurse phoned my parents and asked them to come to the school to take Marc home because he was sick with a headache. Poor little Marc would vomit and cry in pain. Gram lovingly put him to bed, placed an icepack on his head, gave him some aspirin, and pulled the blinds, but that did little to help him feel better. He would sob in agony for hours. Throughout his young years and into high school his headaches persisted. *Why is there so much pain? This poor kid...my heart breaks for him.* We took him to a multitude of specialists who performed every test available. He had Cat Scans and MRIs. Nothing remarkable. He had brain scans. All normal. He met with a mental health counselor. What can we do for him beyond ice packs, pain pills, therapists, and darkened rooms??? *God, it's so hard to watch my guy be this sick. Please help him find relief from his pain and fear.* Suffering throughout his life, he lived more than half the days of each month in that horrid mix of nauseating spiky visual auras, and excruciating pain. The medical community did not offer any help to him beyond prescribing pain pills.

Marc was a bright, shining star, filled with wonder, awe, and surprises on the rare occasion when he wasn't in pain. Marc was on a mission to bring happiness to everyone he met. He loved being around people who treated him kindly, always searching for a safe place to "be". Marc was a compassionate social butterfly who tried to leave his pain behind when he had fun with the people that cared about him. Marc had a heart full of joy, especially when he was free of the headache pain. But his pain came too frequently.

We all yearned for each of Marc's days to be headache-free and took every opportunity in life to have fun while the getting was good. For our family, the happiest places in the world were amusement parks. Those parks that we visited were wonderful escapes for us. We loved everything that made parks magical… the rides, the food, the lights, the parades, and the music. The wilder the ride, the happier we would be. We all adored the old-fashioned, creaky, wooden roller coasters…the body snappers that gave us a rush. *I can still see the smiles on our faces as our coaster came rolling back into the depot. Priceless!* Sadly, as much as he relished riding into the night, there were times when Marc's migraines continued to haunt him even when he was out with family, enjoying himself and having fun. There was no rhyme or reason for the onset of his headaches. Chronic anxiety plagued him all his life as he feared the onset of yet another head-buster. His days of pain prevented him from attending many social events and school activities with friends.

Happily, Marc discovered a new interest that he enjoyed…scouting! It afforded Marc the opportunity to become actively involved with his new scouting buddies and helped him to feel included for the first time in his life. His troop's mission was to help others in the community by doing projects that made their lives easier. Marc lapped up these scouting projects like a kitten drinking warm milk and immediately connected to those activities that helped other people and made our planet a better place. His khaki sash held over forty merit badges given for excellence in all the new skills he learned and projects he completed. Marc yearned to be outdoors and free, and scouting afforded him that opportunity. Mother Nature and Marc were best friends, and he was keen to be out hiking, camping, swimming, and canoeing in the fresh air.

Marc looked forward to the yearly summer camp out in the mountains like a child who looks forward to a visit from Santa Claus. At the campground each year, Marc participated in and won the athletic competition, which included swimming one mile across the lake, biking a mile, and running a mile in immediate succession. Earning the first place winner for this endeavor five times was quite a feat for our young man, who quickly rose through the ranks of scouting. Marc later persevered to attain the highest rank in scouting when he became an eagle scout. Not only did Marc attain the status of eagle scout, but his accomplishments ushered in statewide recognition as he was awarded The Pennsylvania Eagle Scout of the Year. That award ceremony was amazing, and we were so proud of Marc when the committee told us that they knew they had found their number one eagle scout as soon as they read Marc's resume! Scouting was perfect for Marc. His accomplishments gave him a feeling of mastery and fulfillment which expanded his world when he realized how his efforts helped so many others.

    Seemingly less stressful than his grade school years, his moments spent in high school were filled with academic awards, concerts, and proms. He never shared any disturbing times that he may have encountered. Hopefully, there were none, but I highly doubted that. After graduation, Marc left to continue his education at a prestigious college about ninety minutes away from home. Adjusting to campus life, Marc graduated after four years. But during his high school and college years, he couldn't shake the migraines.

    He hated always being sick in bed, so Marc made every moment count whenever he was pain-free. Every Halloween, Marc drove home from college with a bunch of his college buddies and friends, and we hosted his annual pumpkin-carving party. It became our wonderfully anticipated tradition during his four years away at school. Like cotton candy on a stick when you turned it in the drum, this party grew and rapidly became THE Halloween party of the year! *I always look forward to being together with all these kids. We always have a ball.* I baked my famous autumn maple leaf sugar cookies with orange and yellow sprinkles and we ate pepperoni pizzas with double cheese. We also drank gallons of apple cider. The kids' favorite crunchy snack was the roasted salted, greasy pumpkin seeds straight out of the oven!

One year Marc brought two exchange students from Ireland, who had never carved a pumpkin in their lives. I wish you could have heard those girls squeal when they stuck their hands into a squishy pumpkin for the very first time. We all doubled over in laughter. *Whoa! I will never forget the look on their faces when they touched the pumpkin gunk! They looked as if they had just grabbed a pile of buffalo poop!* They shared that they have no pumpkins in Ireland, so they carve faces in gourds for Halloween! *Poor gals didn't know what they were in for!* I appreciated the time we spent with that sweet bunch of guys and gals, and I always awaited next year's Halloween Party with eager anticipation and twenty-five more pumpkins!

Marc was full of joy on the days when he was migraine-free. If there was a good time to be had, he was there, and I'd bet twenty bucks that he was the chief party planner. Wherever the action was, Marc was right in the middle. *He has charisma.* He loved his friends to whom he was deeply devoted. Marc never met a stranger and had a wonderfully magnetic personality. I can still see him out on the dance floor at our wedding reception when Denny and I married. He was the only one out there…dancing and singing the music to the "Chicken Dance" after the dance band left. Within seconds, the dance floor was as active as a beehive. He got everybody out of their seats and onto the floor, dancing the night away. *He's like a magician! He's always so full of life. He's so like his godfather.*

People have said that a baby boy takes after his godfather, and a baby girl takes after her godmother. This was so true for our family. My English teacher godmother was a sweet, demure, letter-writing cousin whom I adored. *She wears cashmere sweaters with pearls! So chic in the 50s!* Although I was always a trendsetter... demure I wasn't. We were both attractive intellectuals who loved to write. Her letters to me were cause for excitement. *I guess when you're young it's nice to get mail and feel like an adult!* We must have written each other a hundred letters back and forth, and I loved to peep into the mailbox for those envelopes with my name and address inscribed in beautifully flowing cursive handwriting. We shared the same energy and the same love for writing. *Remarkably, I'm my godmother's twin.*

    Similar to my godmother and me, Marc followed in his godfather's footsteps. Marc's godfather was my favorite fun-loving pharmacist cousin, and Marc reminded me of him all the time. They were both always teasing and laughing. Having fun flowed through their veins. *I'll always remember how they loved to party and live life to the fullest in their own "grabbin'-for-happiness" ways. Birds of a feather, for sure!* They were more alive than any other people that I knew. These good guys enjoyed living to the max and their energy was as expansive as the entire Universe. They were both generous and compassionate men with hearts wider than the ocean. When Marc's godfather died at a young age, the visitation line that circled the funeral home never ended until ten o'clock at night for two days. One after the other, the multitude of mourners told me how wonderful my dear cousin had been to them. They said that they could call him in the middle of the night and he would get out of bed and drive downtown to his drug store, fill their prescription, and deliver their medicines in the darkness to their home in another town. I heard story upon story of the caring and giving ways of my cousin. People were touched by him and he lifted them and shined his light on them. That's why I loved him so... my heart recognized him as the Light Worker that he was. *He reminds me of Marc. They both have hearts of gold.* I was sure that there were even more wonderful stories of loving-kindness that I didn't even know about. Both men kept their generosity to themselves.

Joy Elaine Reed

The one memory of Marc that fills my heart with joy is our common connection to rainbows. Marc's life was one of color (especially orange) and rainbows. Colors brought us both to a place of peace. *My favorite time with Marc is sitting in his living room in awe of the beautiful rainbows the sunshine cast on the walls, lamps, furniture, rugs, our hands and arms, and even on the dogs!* He had at least ten large crystals hanging in his windows that would throw rainbows throughout his house when the sun peaked out on a rainy day. His home became a "happier-than-an-amusement-park" house when the rainbows were all aglow. *I love the rainbows and the happy memories they bring to me.* We were both always searching for the rainbows in life because we felt peace among the colored hues. Rainbows were our signs that better days were ahead and that even though some days challenged us to the max, life was still good. You'll always find a rainbow between the dark clouds and the light. That's a rainbow's job... to shine its light in the dark sky to remind us that everything needs to be in balance. One year for my birthday present, Marc gave me a round, plastic rainbow maker that I stuck on my window. When the sun shone in, it formed an awesome huge arch of rainbow colors on the dining room floor. In my birthday card, Marc wrote; "You gotta have rainy days to make a rainbow... I love you and wish you rainbows always." Rainbows were our sign of hope.

Party-hardy rainbow-hunter Marc made dark days light for more people than I can count and many more people that I don't even know. He went out of his way to make people happy and lighten their lives. He always gave to others what he, himself, needed the most. Marc was good to everyone. He was constantly there for me and my husband Denny, and he knew that he could count on us to be there for him. My brain locked into the fun times we spent with him...those bright days without headaches, filled with rainbows, carved pumpkins, and the "Chicken Dance". *I love to hear his laughter and not his crying.* It was unfortunate that Marc had wrapped his physical and emotional pain around himself like a sweater that is worn under a bulky winter coat. During his life, I tried many ways to help him, but he put a screen between us and continued on his journey. Marc was Marc, and deep inside he knew what he needed. What was most beautifully unusual was that Marc always had a sweet knowing smile on his face, even when his world was crumbling down all around him.

Joy Elaine Reed

CHAPTER 8

THE PRICE OF FREEDOM

It puzzled me when Marc immediately moved out on his own after his college graduation. We lived in a spacious five-bedroom home and Marc could have stayed here with us while he saved his money. *Why's he moving out? He has all the room in the world in this house!* It didn't make sense to me at all. I asked him why he was leaving, and he just said that it was time for him to move away. He had found a small basement apartment to rent about one mile from our home. I gave him a few chairs and a table, some dishes, and whatever else he needed, and I sewed a pair of drapes for the only small window in his apartment. He called us on the phone often and it was good to connect with him frequently. I sensed a bit more contentment in his voice. But, that contentment was to be short-lived.

I'll never forget the call he made to us about a month after he moved away. I picked up the phone to hear him crying hard. His cries seemed to be unending. "Marc, what's the matter? Honey, are you okay? Do you need us for anything?"

He took a long time to finally find words. Through his sobs, I heard him say, "Yeah, I'm all right." He started crying harder now. "Mom, I have to tell you something, and… I don't know if I can say it to you right now." More crying and sobbing came from the phone receiver.

I was scared to death that he was in deep trouble... that something awful had happened... "Marc, what's the matter? You can tell me anything, you know that. What do you need, honey? What's wrong?" I heard him take a hard gasping breath.

"Mom... the sobbing sounded louder now. It took him a while to speak. "I'm... gay".

I froze in my chair. My mouth hung open. We had known of Marc's specialness since he was a very young child, but the news still left me as stunned as if I had been hit between the eyes by a one-hundred mile-per-hour fastball. Marc's pronouncement made it official. *Marc is gay. It pains him so much to tell you. How long have you seen him feeling uncomfortable in his own skin? He is struggling with being gay. He was born gay and didn't pick being gay. Who picks being gay? Who would pick abuse and torment? Hey, this doesn't change his love for you or your love for him.* As these thoughts rushed through my head, it took me a couple of minutes to regain my composure. *He's still your baby, and nothing will change that.* "It's okay, Marc," I said as tears started streaming down my face. "It's okay." There was silence on his end. I didn't know if he was still listening or if he had passed out.

"I love you, Mom," he said between his sobbing to validate his feelings for me and because he needed approval.

"I love you, too, Marc...no matter who you are. You will always be my baby. I love you unconditionally and I always will. I will always be here for you." I meant every word. *I will never stop loving you.*

Marc cried and thanked me and said that he would talk with me tomorrow. We both ended the call by saying "I love you." When I hung up the phone, I felt like I was enclosed in a pounding MRI machine. Bang, bang, bang went through my head and I had trouble catching my breath. Then I heard Spirit say to me, *"IT'S OKAY. MARC IS WHO HE IS. HE HAS NOT CHANGED OVERNIGHT. NOTHING HAS CHANGED. HE IS STILL THE SAME MARC THAT YOU LOVE."*

Hearing Marc say "gay" brought out so many crazy feelings within me. Hearing "gay" is different from hearing the words, "wreck" or "cancer" or "divorce". Those are events. They are things that happen to a person. Gay is gay... it's a state of being. It can't be changed or erased or given a spin, nor should it be. In a good way, I was truly happy because Marc was finally able to break free of the lies he held within. Coming out gave him the courage to finally be who he always knew he was in his soul. I was glad because I knew that he was relieved to have told his family who he was. But, I hated that my son was gay because in reality, being gay coaxed the hatred out of others, and I was angry because I didn't want to see him become hurt anymore. I knew that the extreme hate he had encountered all his life would escalate in the future. I was furious that my son had been suffering abuse for so long. I was enraged that he was the victim of haters. I was frustrated and angry because I couldn't help Marc combat hate. *I am so afraid for him.* I felt like stealing a truck and running over all the haters that made Marc's life hell. I wanted to kill all the people who hurt other people. *My thoughts are dark and crazy. What's goin' on with me?* I didn't understand what was happening with my wild feelings. I pushed my intense anger into the deepest recesses of my being and chained it to the wall like it was a horrible criminal. I couldn't let it out...if I did, I might have killed myself or the person standing next to me. *Settle down, honey. I can't get angry. Everything's okay. It's all good.*

Trying with all the strength left in me, I couldn't face reality anymore. I didn't have the energy to deal with my son who was gay. I loved him with all my heart but knew "Gay" would be a major issue. I had too many issues happening in my life. I wanted to throw a heavy blanket over my head and all the deranged feelings and thoughts that were twisting around in my brain. My heart was already crushed by the recent death of my dad who was my hero. That was eight months after the neurosurgeons who operated on my dad at two in the morning said the word "cancer" to Mom and me. I took a sabbatical leave from teaching and took care of Dad while he slowly died from a rare form of lymphoma in his spinal cord. I ached to see him unable to walk as cancer rose up his spine. During his last days, he had dementia when cancer reached his brain. He and Mom both "checked out" when they heard the word "cancer". Dad was in shock until he crossed over, he was so afraid. Mom couldn't deal with seeing the love of her life suffer, so his care was deferred to me while she made him delicious homemade dinners which I'm sure she thought would cure him. I knew no meatloaf had that kind of power. Dad died and my world fell apart. That's when I checked out, too.

About a year after Dad died, my mom could no longer live alone because she suffered from emphysema and osteoporosis, so Gram came to live with us. She was in a wheelchair and on constant oxygen, and I couldn't take more time off from work. So I hired a caregiver for Mom during the day while I taught school full-time and took care of her at night. Marc and Adam's dad continued to work two jobs, and I had no brothers or sisters to help me. Every day, I was teaching, taking care of two boys, in charge of all the housework and cooking, and taking care of all Mom's needs. I was also (in my spare time!!!!) an interior designer with a business to run. Mom was in such pain, that when I drove her to a doctor's visit, it took her a half hour to get into the car, inch by inch. There were no internet doctor visits at that time. I was totally alone on this journey. All this concern and caregiving caused confusion that built up and left me beyond tired, frustrated, mad, crazy, and angry. Nothing made sense anymore. I wanted to die. *Things just keep getting worse.* That's when I heard life talk to me…" Oh, no… life ain't done with you yet. It can always get worse. Just you wait!" *Life sucks big time.* I made an appointment with a therapist. I knew that I couldn't sort out these insane feelings alone. *This is all too much for me to carry. My brain feels like it's melting inside my skull and nothing is making sense. I don't have the energy to worry about anybody else right now. I gotta get some help.* And I did. Again.

At that time when Marc came out, it was not easy being gay. *It's never easy being gay. Not feeling part of the crowd. Being alienated. Being different. Being a target for haters.* At the time, being gay had still been treated as a major hushed family secret to be gossiped about behind closed doors while the tips of cigarettes glowed brightly as the smoke filled the room. Although more gays were now slowly coming out of the closet like moths that had eaten their share of an expensive wool sweater, gay life was still a struggle, to say the least. Marc had emerged from the closet, but his revelation and disclosure did not make his circumstances any easier. Marc never acknowledged that it was okay to be different because he had always been told otherwise. I understood Marc but knew that not everyone else would. Marc had to sort things out while he clawed his way through life. As a mother, I was worried because gay-bashing had become an epidemic! *He's been through enough already!*

Being gay wasn't a selected path, although some people acted as if it was a choice. Being gay had never been a choice. Who would choose constant discrimination, violent hate crimes, and laws that denied equality? *Being gay is such a great battle. I can't believe that people think that a person would choose to be gay. Who would ever pick the horrid abuse, trauma, and vicious hate? Nobody would. Go and look into the mirror and try to change the color of the skin on your face. You can't. You are born with the skin you have. Marc didn't choose gay, Marc was gay from day one. He doesn't feel a part of this world, although he tries so hard to fit in. You can't put a square peg in a round hole no matter how hard you try.*

The day that Marc came out did not change who he always had been. I knew Marc and loved him for who he was. *I've finally learned that we all must realize that no matter how we appear to others, we all have a heart that steadily beats, and red blood pulsing through our veins. I hate to think that hearing the word "gay" changes our love for that wonderful person whom we have loved throughout their entire lives. "Gay" is just a word, and it changes nothing. People are gay and have been since the dawn of time. People are gay before they are born. Gay, straight, big, little, brown, white, green, or fuchsia... we are all energy beings of love and nothing will change this. Ever. Having a compassionate heart is all that matters in life. The rest is an illusion.*

One night, at about one o'clock in the morning, the phone rang. I knew this wasn't good news. Marc was on the line. He was crying and screaming at the same time and I couldn't understand a word he was saying. *Dear Lord, now what?* "Honey, what's the matter? Take a deep breath... Are you okay?" It was obvious that he was not all right. That evening, he had been out and about with friends. As he drove home alone from the city, he stopped for a red light. An unknown driver pulled his car up next to Marc's passenger side, pointed a gun, and repeatedly shot directly into the front seat and steering wheel, aiming for Marc. He shattered Marc's windshield and windows and left him for dead as he sped off. Glass was everywhere. Remarkably, not one bullet hit Marc, and he wasn't cut or hurt by the broken glass. He was unharmed! Archangel Michael and his guardian angels had their protective wings around Marc, and I was sure of that! I thanked God and the angels that Marc had not been hurt physically. Mentally and emotionally, neither he nor we would ever be the same. Marc was alone and hysterical. I called the police. *Oh, dear Lord. Marc was at the wrong place at the wrong time...sitting waiting for the light to turn green. What more can this guy go through? Now people are trying to kill him!!! This experience can never be erased from our minds! Ever! Can we just stop all this terrible hate? God, please help us all.*

For a long time after that incident, I called Marc twice every day to make sure that he was doing okay. I asked him to come back home and stay with us for a while. He didn't accept the invitation. He was fragile and shaken by the murder attempt, and was trying his best to live one day at a time. Strangely, something about that horrible incident kept tapping me on the shoulder. *Why did this happen to him?* The next day I realized that Marc had a rainbow bumper sticker on his rear fender. The next time we talked,

Marc with a "C" - Hope from the Hereafter

I asked him if he thought "advertising" was a good idea. *It's not safe out there, honey. Haters are gonna hate.* He told me directly and assertively that he would never remove that bumper sticker because he had every right to be who he was. His determined response made me realize his truth. *Oh Lord, he's right. He's absolutely right. We all have a right to be who we are as long as we don't harm anyone. Marc's entitled to the freedom to be who he is, without any repercussions. Marc has the right to be who he is and receive equal protection under the law. We all are!! My heart aches to know that Marc will always be a target for hate.* The next day I arranged for Marc to work with a counselor and he thanked me.

Marc became the Joan of Arc of his time and stood up for loving-kindness, truth, and compassion. Those were the values for which he searched all his life. *We are all beings of pure love. We are all made from the same source of love... that loving God that resides in every church, synagogue, temple, chapel, and mosque... the God of the trees and flowers and birds...the God of the light, and the God of the Universe.* Marc ached to have peace in this new world he chased after, where everyone loved each other as the same and respected each other's identities. *We are all children of God, no matter what we look or act like. All cracked eggs have yellow yokes, no matter what they look like on the outside.* Bringing the world together to live as one became Marc's passion. I was afraid that Marc's life would become much more difficult now that he became the champion for human rights, but I knew that nothing would stop him from fighting for his cause. I applauded his fierce courage, but feared for his safety. *Marc has every right to be Marc. He gets it. He knows what life is all about. Love is all there is. Please, angels, keep him safe. We are all tired of living in fear.*

Many jobs were lost because Marc walked out, unable to take the verbal abuse from his bosses who taunted and insulted him for being gay. *How can a boss humiliate Marc in front of all his co-workers? Who does that?* Marc was like me, he was a peacemaker. "Live and let live" was his motto. Neither Marc nor his brother Adam could be deliberately mean to anyone. That was just not programmed into their DNA. *I am so frustrated. I don't know how much more we can take.* Although he avoided drama like the plague, it followed him around like a looming, end-of-the-day shadow that he couldn't escape... and Marc's headaches continued to haunt him.

CHAPTER 9

ANOTHER LIFETIME

"Many gay men are highly intuitive." I heard that statement from a lovely woman who is a wonderful psychic medium and a dear friend. She was correct. Marc was very tuned-in. Although everyone is blessed with psychic gifts, Marc and I were awake to their presence and our intuitive abilities were active. *Everybody on this Earth has psychic abilities, whether they believe it or not.* For Marc and me, our psychic gifts kicked in at birth.

Marc and I were very close. We read each others' minds, and telepathically connected to each other's energy, and we had done so all our lives. *It is uncanny how we know what each other is thinking.* My ringtone for Marc's incoming calls on my cell phone was a happy little ditty called "By the Seaside". Without knowing that, guess what ringtone he picked for me on his phone? *That's just crazy! Our connection is so strong that we finish each other's sentences!*

Growing up, I had a strong connection with my mother, just like I had with Marc. When I was away in college, without a phone call from my parents, I knew every single time that Mom and Dad would plan a long drive up for a visit with me. I'd arrange ahead of time to clear my schedule on that day. It was uncanny and continued that way for all my college years! And, after I was married, every evening, without knowing it, I cooked the same dinner as my mother cooked. I'd call her from school each day at lunchtime to check how her day was going, and I'd ask her what she was cooking for supper. "Pork chops and Spanish rice." *What??...that's what I'm making in my slow cooker!* Chili, stuffed cabbage, roast beef, or WHATEVER... this saga continued every day for twenty years! It never failed! And Marc cooked the same meals as me, too! *This is too wild. Nobody would believe this!* We never compared our psychic gifts, but we realized that our intuitive abilities tied us together with a big purple bow of awareness.

When I was a senior in college, I decorated the metal door that opened into my cramped dorm room with posters, photos, and all kinds of crazy, wild things that I liked. My door became a giant collage. *I'll always hold dear that huge poster with a closeup of my favorite actor's gorgeous face that I placed front and center. Be still my heart!* In between many other pictures, I also taped up a large magazine page with three words written in huge letters... "ORANGE IS ZIP". *Why?... I didn't know at the time.* The black letters were printed on a white background. I can't remember if it was an ad or a title for an article, and I don't know why it appealed to me. I liked the color orange, but it never thrilled me. I remember that, after it was decorated, I took a photo of my door. That photo froze the energy of that precise moment as it etched a memory into my mind. Photos are energy extenders. *I will always remember my "ORANGE IS ZIP" door. It was just so cool!* I didn't know why I hung up that meaningless sign, or did I?

Five years later, Marc was born, and he turned his world into the energy of orange. All his life, he was tuned into orange's vibration. It's the color of the second energy center of our bodies and the color of passion, joy, and sexuality. Marc lived in an orange world. It must have comforted him. The color orange probably helped him embrace his sexuality and gave him a sense of meaningfulness in this world. Orange socks, orange jackets, orange shirts, orange pots and pans, orange everything! You could spot him in a crowd because he glowed with the color of naval oranges. *If it's orange, it's Marc! I must have known about my "orange guy" five years earlier when I hung that sign on my door! Crazy wild!*

Marc with a "C" - Hope from the Hereafter

One hot summer day, Marc and I were relaxing in our home at the beach, sitting in the cool shade of the front porch, enjoying the tranquility and the sweet aroma of gardenias. I shared an event that happened the night before while I was asleep. I excitedly mentioned to Marc that I had "traveled" with my guardian angel during the night. Now, Marc "got" my psychic abilities. We knew we were both intuitive. We had always shared so many things telepathically, so I figured it was okay to continue my story... "My guardian angel took me by the hand and led me through the air. Everything I saw was in brilliant colors. We flew about a hundred yards above the ground for a while, and then, in the distance, I saw a brown barn next to a little wooden shack. I felt like I was in the Midwest, and I could see that everything was covered in sand. This scene seemed like it took place during the Dust Bowl. The next thing I knew, I was down on the Earth, standing directly in front of the barn. I was alone and I looked down at my feet. They were little and my socks and shoes were dirty. I felt like I was in the body of a little girl. I felt as if I were seven years old.

The sand was blowing every which way, and I could feel it pelting me in the face as I stood in front of the barn, trying my best to open the huge barn door into the punishing wind. I had sand on my lips and grit in my mouth. I finally pushed my way inside the barn and then the door loudly slammed behind me with a big bang. I was holding a round basket made of wood hollowed out from a tree stump, with a blue-checked homespun cloth placed inside. The only light in the dark barn came from the cracks between the wooden boards in the walls. I walked around in the barn and called to our little chicken. We only had one skinny chicken left, and we didn't want to eat her today for fear we would need to cook her in a couple of days to ward off starvation. I looked in her nest, and it held only one egg that I put into my basket. I was hoping that Mother wouldn't be disappointed. I knew that we would share that single egg for dinner tonight. My stomach growled all the time anymore, and I was starving.

As I left the barn with the egg, I understood that we were living in desperate times, and I knew what was coming. I shoved the barn door open enough so that I could slide out, and it didn't need to open much because I was so thin. I lowered my head as I pushed through the dust-filled whirlwinds, and ran toward the house, hoping the wind wouldn't lift me into the air. My dress blew up around my neck, and I couldn't even see our house because of the sand in my eyes. Fighting the raging dust storm, I finally made it to our two-room shack. There was a wooden bench on the small front porch, and a clay jug under the one window in the front. Everything on the porch was covered with sand.

I opened the door to our little house and walked directly to the left side of the main front room where we cooked and ate. I saw a small rectangular table made of pine and two oak chairs that were pushed under the tabletop. There was a warming fire in the fireplace which was built in the center of the back wall. Next to the stone fireplace on the right was an oak rocking chair. My grandmother's cedar chest, which held most of our belongings, was next to the rocker. We put a quilt on top of this chest so that we could use it as a seat. I saw an open doorway that led to the only bedroom in the back of the house.

The shack was tiny, but it felt so safe and warm. Mother was standing by a kitchen sink on the far left and in her hands, she held a towel made from a white flour sack. My mother and I were the only two left living in the house. The rest of the family was gone. Mother had a smile on her face. She was so loving. I could feel her love energy from far away. We loved each other dearly. Her love for me made me feel that everything would be all right, no matter what happened next."

I paused, and surprisingly, this time MARC continued... "I watched you walk into the house with your basket. I had been washing a dish and I stood next to the sink. I wore a gray dress with tiny pink flowers, and an apron made from a clean brown feed sack. My drab, dark brown hair had flecks of gray, and it was waist length and braided down my back. You wore a red gingham dress, and your hair was tied back with a blue ribbon. When you left the house to get the egg, you got sand in your dark blond hair. We were both very thin and weak, and our energy was lagging.

There was a fire in the fireplace and the house felt so cozy. You had a frown on your face when you brought me the only egg that you collected, and I hugged you and told you how much I appreciated you and our lone chicken. I fried that egg with some lard in a heavy cast-iron skillet and I gave you a spoonful. We had eaten nothing but eggs and an occasional chicken for months, but we were so grateful that we had any food at all. Our garden was long gone. We ate slowly, making the meal last so that we would feel less hungry later. It was just you and me together, trying to make it work. We knew that tomorrow we would have to eat our last chicken. That would be the end of all our food. The only things we had left were the house and the barn. There was nowhere to go and no way to get there. That didn't matter. We had each other. We had love. We also knew that in a few days we were both going to die."

Hearing this, I felt as if I had fallen from the top of the tallest building in the world and my body soon would splatter on the sidewalk. My head was swirling. I was stunned. *What? Are you kidding me? I can't believe this! You're right!! You saw the whole thing! Oh, Lord... you were there! You were my mother! How did you know all this?* I was astounded that he finished my story! *You shared my dream. No...you shared another lifetime with me! Holy smoke, that's incredible!* I looked at Marc in astonishment. I asked him how he knew. He told me, "I don't know, I just did."

This incredible experience was my validation that life is eternal and that our souls go on forever. We were all part of a large soul tribe that experiences lifetimes together. Marc had been my mother, and I had been his child in another life! It was amazing to have lived this past-life scenario with Marc. *I can't believe this! This is wild!* I didn't know just how many lifetimes we had shared together, but I did know that we had dearly loved each other before this go around on Earth and that death no longer held fear for me.

Joy Elaine Reed

CHAPTER 10

MARC WITH A "C"

Everybody who knew Marc referred to him as Marc with a "C". One day, he shared the funniest story... he and his friends went to a coffee house, and Marc, being kind and generous as usual, bought everyone coffee. The barista wrote each person's name on their cup. Marc told the barista that his name was Marc with a "C". Marc got his cup of coffee, laughed like crazy, took a picture of it, and posted a photo on social media... the barista had written "CARK" on his cup. *LOL... Are you serious?* To this day we all still laugh at that story, and now our Marc with a "C" is also known to family and friends as "Cark"!

My friend Cindy came to visit with us one day and happened to meet Marc for the first time while he was staying with us at the beach. Of course, he introduced himself as Marc with a "C", and he showed her the photo of his coffee cup that he had posted on social media, and told her, "Just call me Cark". He also gave her a new seashell keychain that he had just bought for himself at the beach store. He was always sharing with others, and Cindy got a kick out of that and never forgot their first meeting and the bright energy of Cark. From that day forward, she kept her pool key on the keychain Cark gave to her, and they remained fast friends.

Cindy is a strong and amazing woman who is on a mission to brighten peoples' lives by sending them uplifting cards, notes, and letters. *She has no idea how her cards encourage me and help me heal. If everybody would do this, the world would be a better place.* She and her husband had been so caring and compassionate towards us, especially after Marc left the world. They had lost their son a couple of years before Marc died, so they knew and lived the same heartbreak as Denny and I. Better friends you would be hard-pressed to find. One day we received a card in the mail from Cindy. The card was one of countless messages of love she had sent us, helping us to keep the faith through our trials. The card read as follows:

Dear Joy and Denny,
  Thinking of you and had to share a story...
  We live in a new neighborhood, so we're forever meeting someone new...well, Pete went out to get our mail and met the neighbor moving in across the street from us.
  Pete says, 'Hi! I'm Pete and my wife is Cindy"...now wait, this is where Marc comes in on the story...
  'Hi!' She says..."My name is Caren (Karen) with a C! " LOL All I could think of was Marc with a "C"...LOL
  Love you, Cindy XO

That was such a sweet story for Cindy to share and it helped me call to mind such wonderful memories. Cindy and Pete will always be a part of our family. We called them our "hurricane forever friends" because we stayed with them in their well-protected house with a generator and boarded windows during some of the huge hurricanes that threatened us at the beach. And there's a SPIRIT story attached to our first hurricane encounter with them…
  In 2016, a ferocious hurricane name Matthew threatened our coast and loomed closer day by day. Watching the weather forecast made me nauseous and as wired as if I had just drunk thirty cups of regular dark-roast coffee. We first heard about this on Monday, and Matthew was due to impact our coastline on Friday,

and it appeared more gigantic and troublesome as I watched the weather reports each day. Knowing that I could cancel my reservation at any time, I called a hotel in Laurinburg, North Carolina, on Monday and booked a room for three nights for the end of the week. Now, I had never been to Laurinburg in my life, but I knew that it was a couple of hours inland from the coast and would probably afford us safe shelter if we had to evacuate. It felt like the right thing to do at the time. We had never before evacuated during a storm... we usually just pulled all the porch furniture into the living and dining rooms and held a hurricane party as we dodged around the furnishings in the dark. But this storm seemed different and more destructive. *This is no time to party!* Matthew looked ominous and deadly and was headed straight for us.

  I had to pack clothes and essentials into our suitcases. I searched the house for important papers that we needed. I had valuables to gather, and many other tasks to complete before the storm hit. We tied the porch furniture down with bungee cords and brought all the accessories and potted plants inside before we left. We had to remember to pack our medications. My mind spun in circles, making hurricane adjustments and plans. Our water needed to be turned off. I froze bottles of water and stuck them into the freezer hoping to keep it as cold as possible so at least our frozen food could be saved if our power went off while we were gone. I filled the bathtub with water in case we needed it to flush the toilets if we stayed and didn't have water. My brain was running overtime and was burning up!

  If you remained at the beach during a mandatory evacuation, you did so without the benefit of first responders or emergency medical teams. You were on your own. Forget calling 911. *Hurricanes are hazardous to your mental health!! Talk about anxiety.... You ain't lived until you've lived through a hurricane!* As Matthew intensified, Cindy called on Wednesday evening and invited us to stay at their home which was located about 10 miles inland. There, we would be safely out of any destructive storm surge on the coast. We knew we had to leave, and we appreciated their concern, but we did not want to burden anybody with our presence. I thanked her and told her that I had booked a room in North Carolina. She told me that their offer would still stand if we changed our minds.

That Thursday, our car was packed and we were ready to leave our home. I walked back into our house to make sure everything was unplugged. *Really? If our house blows away, it won't matter what's unplugged!* I walked into our bedroom and saw Denny sitting on the bed and putting on his shoes. Both our stomachs were tied in knots. As I walked toward Denny, I "heard" the words..."*DON'T GO TO LAURINBURG.*" My energy immediately got as heavy as mud, and I felt like I was sinking in quicksand. "*DO NOT GO TO LAURINBURG*"... I heard it again and knew that we must do what Spirit was telling us to do. I told my husband that we shouldn't go to Laurinburg. He said, "Why? You've already booked a room there. Let's just go there. Where else can we go?" I told him that we could go to Pete's house. He didn't agree, but I wasn't taking "No" for an answer. I called Cindy and Pete and asked them if their offer was still good. Fifteen minutes later we were away from the coast, safely staying in a beautiful home with boarded windows, and we felt relieved being there with our friends.

Our pre-hurricane time with them that night was priceless. They were so delightful to be with and their hospitality alleviated much of our storm anxieties. We watched movies and we felt at home. *Cindy pampers the heck out of Denny, serving apple slices with caramel sauce for an evening snack! Cindy, you're making me look bad here!* We always had fun together. Then, in the middle of the night, we knew that Category-Four Matthew had arrived. We had lost power. Matthew had impacted the shore. In the morning, when we peered outside it was as dark as night and as we sat together in the blackness, we could hear the pine trees snapping outside our boarded windows. We were grateful we were not outside where the wind was howling as it bent the palm trees to the ground and the streets overflowed with water. The next day, we hunkered down in Cindy's walk-in closet many times when the hurricane-triggered tornadoes ripped up the land about a half-mile away from their home. *That's way too close for comfort!* Although it was a horrifying experience, we felt safe with Pete and Cindy. *At least we're not all alone in an unknown town.*

Late that second afternoon we heard the shocking news on our battery-powered radio... the city of Laurinburg and the surrounding areas had been flooded the night before and were under more than four feet of water! They had no power... no food... no water... nothing! Cars were stranded in the flood water and couldn't start. Everything in that town was silenced by the storm. Laurinburg had been devastated. Matthew had ravaged the city. Later, we heard horror stories from people who had evacuated the beach and had gone to Laurinburg and were trapped by the floodwaters. *Whoa, Spirit had kept us safe with Pete and Cindy! Oh, my Lord! We are so blessed! Thank you, Spirit, Archangel Michael, and all our guardian angels!* When we told our kids this story and told them how grateful we were to be safe with Cindy and Pete, they told us how glad they were that we had loving friends at the beach who cared about us and supported us when we needed them. *It's so wonderful to know that we have the support of Spirit, friends, and family, wherever we may be. I don't know where we would be without the support of others! It's so good to know that we can always count on Cindy and Pete in the midst of a storm.*

When faced with a life challenge, we knew that we could also count on our kids. Adam came to our aid many times to help us, and so did Denny's daughter and son. But the gold star went to Marc who became our biggest supporter when Denny and I needed help, no matter where we were living. Marc was our "go-to" who would come to our rescue. He flew down south to our home and assisted us through our countless illnesses and surgeries. He would do anything for me and Denny, whom he adored. He drove us to doctor's offices, hospitals, and physical therapy sessions. He was our home health liaison, transportation specialist, and much more. Realizing that we were electronically challenged, Marc became our technical support guru who hooked us up with cell phones, printers, televisions, computers, I-pads, and the internet. He also knew all the crazy mass of wires and cords behind our TV and which holes they were connected to on all our equipment. *Thank God* We always called on Cark first and he never hesitated to help us.

Marc's life was tough, but Marc was tougher. Through the pain, abuse, and trauma.... Marc endured. Amazingly, as trying as his life was, Marc loved to love. Marc treated everyone with love and respect, which is what he always sought for himself. If you need help, he would give you his last penny and the shirt off his back, even if he didn't know you. Marc was truly an unselfish man with generous and caring ways. Denny's son had once told us, "If Marc with a "C" had a million dollars, he would still be penniless, because he would have given every cent away!" *That's our Cark!*

I truly felt that Marc was an old soul because no other soul would have signed up for his life's journey full of challenges. Knowing that love was the secret ingredient, he wanted to make the world a better place for everyone. He understood that we are all one. Nothing that ever happened to him hampered his love for his close friends and family. "Of course" was the answer he always gave if anyone asked him for a favor and he always found the time to help. He unselfishly gave others what he needed the most. Cark just wanted others to love him because he valiantly tried, but could not find the love in himself. It was such a shame because everybody who knew Marc, loved Marc, and I don't think he ever realized that truth. Was Marc a spiritual being sharing unconditional love?... "Of course!" Cark got it!

Joy Elaine Reed

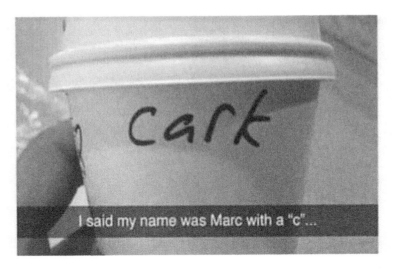

CHAPTER 11

A GOOD PLACE

Although it was shaky and rusty, I trusted that the aluminum chair would hold me, as I mentally wrote "beach chair" at the top of the perpetual shopping list in my mind. I glanced down as I sat on the brightly-colored cartoony fish that swam on the worn canvas, and settled into the seat. I wished that I had worn a heavier jacket. In my bulky fisherman knit sweater I felt a chill, but I expected that in January. After the quick morning downpour, and even with the cool air, the sun glowed in the afternoon sky and warmed my soul like a bowl of my mother's hot vegetable beef soup with homemade noodles. *God bless you, Mom and Dad...I miss you both. We all miss you. You were so good to us.*

This was years earlier, and year number ten of our twenty years living at the beach in South Carolina after my husband Denny and I both retired from teaching. *Oh, this is so nice, sitting at the beach in January!* As seasoned Northerners, we were learning and adjusting to a whole new environment, as if we had just been dropped onto the surface of Jupiter. We traded icy weather for tons of sunshine and "confused tourist" traffic along poorly marked local roads. This day at the beach was nothing like the below zero, cold and snowy Pennsylvania winter days that depleted my energy. *Thank goodness I'm not living there anymore.*

I looked out over the vast water and spotted a couple of young guys jumping in the deep rolling waves as if they were down in the warm ocean off tropical Key West. I laughed and thought

how crazy it was seeing tourists come to South Carolina in the winter, wearing shorts and flip-flops - let alone playing in the ocean. *I used to be like them! I wouldn't do it now on a sure bet. It's too cold for me!*
    As they splashed, a rainbow blazed overhead, and I felt my energy double and my heart sing. *Rainbows rule!* Remembering the many huge, half-circle double rainbows that I spotted outside of our southern cottage, I thanked the South Carolina sky for painting such a colorful portrait of "Roy G Biv" today. Those glowing, multi-hued sky ribbons melted straight into my soul and boosted my energy with joy. For me, there was nothing in this world more satisfying than seeing a rainbow decorate the sky with multicolored bands. I adored rainbows…they were my assurance from Spirit that "It's all good". *Rainbows are God's way of reminding me of my blessings. Nothing can compare! I will never stop being a rainbow hunter!*
    Watching those amusing guys who reveled in the waves, oblivious to the light show above them, ignited memories of my own two sons. I laughed and recalled how people did a double-take when they saw my sons together. As babies, Marc and Adam used to look so much like twins. I couldn't even tell them apart when I looked at their baby pictures! Once when my youngest son, Adam, played the lead in his high school's musical performance, the director tacked up all the baby pictures of the cast members behind the glass onto the bulletin board in the high school foyer. People got a kick out of guessing who the cast members were in those photos. On the opening night, Adam asked me why his brother's photo was posted on the board. *What? Are you kidding me? Did I give Marc's baby picture to the director? I did!* I couldn't believe that even I had a tough time telling them apart when they were young.
    I carried my sons' fun high school days memories around in my mind because those guys and those times were a big part of my life. As if I were filming a video in my mind, I remembered how Adam and his friends danced across the stage. Then, in my memories, I watched Marc confidently singing and dancing in his

high school's musical production. *Oh, what joyful times. This never gets old. These guys can sing!* Both boys were soloists at their high school Christmas concerts, and if I closed my eyes now I could still see them on stage and hear them singing "Silent Night". *Remembering them singing brings me tears of joy! What gifts they both have!* I adored them and I was proud to be their mom, not for what they did, but for who they were. They were wonderful sons. It surprised me that they resembled each other and were alike in so many ways when they were young, but as adults, the five-year age difference created unmistakable changes in these loving brothers. *It's so cool to remember them as young and to see them now. Boy, I'm getting old!*

    The freezing, crazy guys out in the waves took quick, deep strides through the surf to the shore, hit the beach, and wrapped themselves in flimsy beach shop towels decorated with images of busty gals clad in tiny striped bikinis. The guys pointed to the sky as they finally spotted my rainbow. Toweling down and shivering, they threw their heads back to fling the wet hair off their faces. It was crystal clear that they were here on vacation and wanted to get their money's worth. *Would a local be swimming in the icy surf today? I doubt it.* Down the beach the guys ran, wrapped in their towels, and I presumed that they were headed to their hotel, eager to take a hot shower. Watching these guys reminded me of how my sons loved the ocean, and how much I missed being with them.

    Adam now lived in Arizona. Marc still lived in Pennsylvania. They flew here to South Carolina every Christmas and visited us at the beach to celebrate my Christmas Eve birthday. I smiled, thinking that it was so sweet of them to make my birthday and Christmas so special for Denny and me. Living states apart never presented a barrier, and if we ever needed them in any way, or if they ever wanted to be with us, they'd catch a plane and jet here in a heartbeat. They supported us through my husband's open-heart surgery, knee replacements, and countless other challenging operations that set off the alarm systems at every airport on our travels.

Both Adam and Marc were tall, handsome, charming, and kind. They were gifted with insightful intelligence and keen senses of humor. They graduated from college in four years, both in business and marketing. They were good kids. No, good men. I knew how blessed I was to be their mom and I thanked God every day for sending them to me. They were now grown men, making decisions about their lives and living for today. *Where are my sweet babies wrapped in their blankets? Where have the years gone?*

I let my thoughts drift away like a wispy cloud when I spotted a lone pelican out over the waves, diving into the surf for his dinner. Fearlessly, he plunged straight down into the green water and then flew back up into the sky like a yo-yo on a string. After three tries he finally emerged with a big fish hanging from his huge pouch of a mouth. *How many times have I been mesmerized watching these amazing diving birds? This never gets old!* I loved being out in the sunshine, by the ocean, lapping up negative ions and feeling my energy brighten. Being near water did me good. Water raised my energy. And, I couldn't get enough of the South Carolina critters that I loved to watch.

My heart soared one evening as I witnessed the newly hatched baby sea turtles scurry from their sandy nest to the faraway shore. *I still can't believe that I was there, at that exact moment when they exploded out of the nest!* I remembered standing in the dunes when those tiny guys hatched and took off in a flash for the safety of the waves. What a bolt of excitement for me, and a seemingly impossible trek for these strong baby turtles who were used to maneuvering in water, not sand. They were so far from the ocean and had to wiggle across those wide beaches. *That's a heavy job they have to do right after they hatch. But, that's how it works for them. I guess everybody's programmed to do what they gotta do.*

I smiled as I thought about my sweet husband and me enjoying lunch on the deck of our favorite fish joint on the water, while majestic bald eagles glided over the Intracoastal Waterway as we munched on crispy cod bites and fries. Both the locals' and the tourists' jaws dropped as we watched these breathtaking birds fly over our heads. We were so amazed that it never even occurred to us to take a picture! Especially for me, it was such a rush! The nearness of these incredible birds, which are one of my totem animals, brought joy to my heart.

And, while I thought of the beach, the ridiculous brain video that will always be filed away in my mind was the memory of the motionless flounder that I stepped on when I walked in the shallow waves of the beach one hot summer day. *You ain't lived until you've stepped on a sleeping flounder! Whoa! Scared the heck out of me, wiggling under my foot like that!* I just couldn't imagine what was happening. I jumped high enough to touch a cloud and I think people thought I was being attacked by a great white shark. I let out blood-curdling screams as I stood in one foot of water! Confused, I looked down and expected to see the tentacles of an octopus wrapped around my legs. No octopus, but the sand under the water was stirring. I realized that I had stepped on a flounder, but luckily I stepped off him when I jumped up. Without my foot on him, he rippled the sides of his flat body as he quickly glided over the sand, out toward the ocean depths. Now he was safe from other "killer beach walkers"! What the heck are the chances that a flounder would be lying, buried in the sand, on that exact part of the East Coast while I was walking there? *Really? If some big mega-company held a contest that would award the winner fifty million dollars for walking on a flounder in the surf of the Atlantic Ocean, I would never be able to do that again in a zillion years!* I shook my head at the absurdity of it all.

Devastating hurricanes and crazy tourist seasons had never tainted my love for the awesome shore animals, and the magnificent ocean, lakes, and waterways near me. I felt at home with Mother Nature and the animal kingdom of South Carolina. I was in love with the egrets and herons in our backyard lake and the cormorants that dived deep into the water. And the painted buntings at my bird feeders took my breath away and were a joy to behold. The more water and critters that surrounded me, the better I felt.

Joy Elaine Reed

South Carolina was the place that I dearly loved. It was a welcomed change and so different from where I had grown up in the North. I felt happy here. I had the feeling that I had lived a past life here before, and it was good. South Carolina felt like home to me.

In my daily journal, I wrote that I had a lovely repose at the beach today... *It gives me such joy to relax at the beach. It's such a good place to be. Thank you, Spirit. My heart is so grateful for my life, my family, the ocean, and all my blessings, I love South Carolina and I belong here. I will never leave my happy place.*

I was unaware that Spirit had other plans for me.

CHAPTER 12

ANGEL TALK

"Oooooh!! Oooooh, help me!" I cried out as my body hit the floor, feeling as if a cannonball had been shot into my back. I screamed out to Denny for help. The pain was so disabling that I couldn't take a breath. Vomit collected in my throat and I started to choke. Trying to lift me, Denny grabbed my arms and raised me inch by inch. It took him twenty minutes to get me up from the floor. Feeling faint, I was bent over like the number seven. Pain radiated from my shoulders, down my back, and into my legs and feet, and I couldn't take one step. My muscles felt as if they had been torched and ripped off my bones and my veins burned with the fire of boiling liquid steel. How my husband ever got me to the hospital will forever be a mystery to me. *Thank God I have Denny here with me, I don't know what I would do without his help!*

Pain management is for the birds… It never helps me. Who wants to manage pain?
I want this pain to leave my body forever! We had now been at the beach for almost twenty years, and after many years of trying ineffective shots in my back and pelvis, pain pills that made me puke, and torturing physical therapy, my pain management doctor had performed a radio-frequency spinal ablation three months earlier. Using an electrical current to heat up and burn the nerve tissue to stop it from sending pain signals, I was supposed to get at least six months of freedom from the torturing pain of my spinal deformities and the constricting stenosis of my spine. It was not so.

I guess the nerves grew back with a vengeance on this night when I dropped to the floor, unable to move. I couldn't live another day being unable to walk and in constant torment. I was older now and time had taken its toll on my nerves and my back muscles that were weakened by my crippled gait. My legs and feet were becoming numb and my ankles were always swollen. Like a broken matchstick, I was hunched over and bent at a forty-five-degree angle, and I dreaded every step that I took. *I wish I could just pull that sciatic nerve right outta my body!*

My husband rushed me to the hospital as quickly as he could. Having no clue as to why my back went out on me, I just wanted some relief. It seemed to me as if the doctor in the emergency room administered every pain killer known to man to help alleviate the pain in my body. The nurses gave me three medications in my intravenous drip, and tons of pills by mouth. Twenty minutes later they injected long skinny needles with more pain meds into my arms. Nothing seemed to work. The medicine just made me vomit, so they gave me another shot of different medicine to lessen nausea. *I'm ready to pull off my head. Please help me.* I was taken to radiology where I endured a body scan, and I was shocked when they said that the scan was unremarkable, as I was sure that I had somehow broken every bone in my back. An hour later, I started to relax although the pain only lessened from a level of twenty to a level of eighteen! I was still hurting and confused by the quick onset of this horrific episode of excruciating pain. I had never experienced back pain that was so severe and, believe me, I was the poster child for back pain. The doctor sent me home with a couple of prescriptions that I couldn't take because they made me vomit. I couldn't lie in bed, and could only lie on my side on the sofa, although once I got on the sofa, I couldn't get off. I used ice, heat, over-the-counter pain medication, and remedy creams. My back and bottom got burnt from the heating pad that I left on too long. Attempting to trick my pain, I stuck four electrodes from my muscle stimulation unit to my back and legs. This entire routine was as effective as eating soup with a fork. Two days later I couldn't take the pain any longer, so I checked the web, found a neurosurgeon, and made an appointment at his office in North Carolina. I had arrived at the breaking point (literally), and I wanted the opinion of another physician. I somehow "felt" that surgery was the only option for me now.

Two weeks later, I was back in the emergency room, again unable to move. It hurt to even take a shallow breath. Another round of pills and shots awaited me. The emergency room doctor wanted me to stay overnight in the hospital so they could do a different body scan in the morning. *No, no. no!* I did not want to be hospitalized that night and refused because my initial appointment with the neurosurgeon that I had called was the very next day. I was desperate to see him so he could give me some kind of answer. *I gotta see this neurosurgeon tomorrow. I can't live any longer without being able to walk!* I was convinced that only surgery could help me now.

The sun was shining the following morning as we drove past neatly-groomed golf course communities into North Carolina. Luckily, the surgeon's office was a straight shot from South Carolina and not that much of an automotive challenge for my husband who never drove out of town, and rarely drove in town. For the last five years, although I couldn't walk well, I could still drive. My husband hated driving anywhere, so I became our official chauffeur, and he was used to having it easy as I drove down the crowded beach streets filled with out-of-state cars and drivers who were trying to find their destination on poorly marked roads and exits. *Driving through town during tourist season at the beach is an experience unlike any other... I'd rather have cockroaches poured into my jeans! I really wish he would drive every once in a while.*

Fortunately, my husband was driving today and I was glad to be sitting in the passenger seat on our journey to see this neurosurgeon. I wasn't sure if we were headed to the gates of heaven or the gates of hell. We hadn't a clue what to think or expect. We were both quiet during this hour trip... both of us locked in thought, wondering what this neurosurgeon would tell us and if he could help me.

As we drove up the highway, I remembered our last vacation in Italy four years earlier which ended our traveling days, as I could hardly keep up with our patient tour guides. Walking became torture to me, even with my walker or my cane. I rarely left the house now, and if I went to the store, I used the cart to help me walk. When I was home, I felt the mental and physical pain of being unable to amble down our sidewalk to just get the mail. I recounted all the doctors, specialists, chiropractors, acupuncturists, natural healers, pain managers, and physical therapists I had seen throughout my life. I wanted to put my head in my hands and cry when I recalled all the pills, shots, creams, ablations, adaptive equipment, chiropractic adjustments, braces, acupuncture, and exercises that didn't work for me. *I'm so frustrated. I've had it. My disfigured spine is serious business.* As our car sped down the highway, we were both sitting as tight as lassoed calves as we watched the scenery zoom past our windows.

I remember when this back stuff first started.... "Stand up straight", my mother told me as she pinned the hem in my royal blue chiffon dress that I was ready to rock at the Christmas dance. Scoliosis was my great seventh-grade horror... before that day we never noticed the hump on my back because I was so active. My parents immediately took me to a local doctor who ordered X-rays. As he checked the films, he shook his head from left to right and flatly told my parents that I did indeed have scoliosis and that I would have to be in a body cast for one year to stop my bones from growing. *What? Say that again.* I watched the blood drain from Dad's face, and I hoped he could catch Mom who was about to faint straight away. I had pictured myself in my mind, lying on a hospital bed in the living room next to the picture window... for one entire year! *What will my life be as I lie immobile next to that window for three hundred sixty-five days? How am I going to go to the bathroom?* Shock and a million questions entered our minds. This local doctor recommended that we see a spine specialist in the city who could give us more information.

This new neurosurgeon was gentle and kind when he first spoke with us. He was the most well-known doctor in the scoliosis business, and he addressed our concerns compassionately. He stated that no one knows how scoliosis occurs. *Leave it to me to have the mystery affliction!*
He kindly said that he understood the severity of my spinal deformities, as he had dealt with this same problem many times, mostly with females. He ordered x-rays of my back which were taken at his office. Ten minutes later, he pushed my X-ray up under the clip of a large light-box which showed all of my white crooked bones. *My spine looks like a loop-de-loop wooden roller coaster!* After placing a small plastic protractor on my x-ray, he measured the bends in my vertebrae and calmly assured us that he would monitor any change of angles in my spine every month. After one year, my spine had not shown any more curvature, and the idea of placing me in a full-length body cast was moot, as he felt that I had already achieved my adult height (in seventh grade!). We were all relieved, and could finally take a deep breath.

I needed to continue to see this prominent spine specialist once a year until I was twenty-one years old, and had graduated from college. I can still remember Doc telling me that I was five feet, six inches tall, but if my spine were straight, I would have been five feet, eleven inches! *Wow...to think that I could have been a supermodel!* I had shrunk due to a double S curve and a twisted spine. *Sounds like an Olympic high dive from the top platform... "Joy's now performing a Double S Curve with a Twist"! Oh Lord, I'm just glad this is all over.* I never in a million years anticipated any problems down the road.

I went from the pretty girl with a slight hump on her back when she touched her toes, to the old bent-over, crooked witch that grabbed little kids who walked through the woods and tried to eat them for dinner. As I aged, arthritis and stenosis in my spine made my life a daily nightmare. When I stood, it was for less than three minutes, and that was only after I had lifted my right heel and bent my right knee. I had unbearable sciatic pain down my left hip and leg which became numb from my thigh to my toes. Both feet were numb, tingling, and burning as if I was standing on the hot red burners of an electric stove. I felt horrible pain when I took a step, and I thought that my left hip was broken. My height dropped to five feet two inches, and I felt like an incredible shrinking woman. Some muscles shortened, and some muscles lengthened as I became more unbalanced. I fell often. I couldn't walk without a walker, and even then, I could only walk five feet before I needed to sit down. Feeling like a corkscrew, I continued to push myself to do what was necessary to keep active and independent, but it was becoming more difficult for me each day. Back surgery had been recommended a few times because I had suffered from this horrid pain for years. *Who in their right mind raises their hand when back surgery is discussed? This isn't a disc, it's an entire back!* Sadly, although I put it out of my mind in the past, I knew I was ready now. It was time and I had to do this. I had no choice. Surgery was my last hope.

We were shocked when, after body scans, full-spine x-rays, and bone density tests, this North Carolina neurosurgeon whom I embraced to give me hope, said he couldn't help me. *I can't believe what I am hearing! Oh, God...No! NO!* He told us that he would need to operate on my entire spine from my neck to my pelvis, breaking each vertebra and putting in pins, screws, and rods, because I had "rigid scoliosis". He said it was too extreme a procedure for his surgical team in Charlotte, North Carolina, to operate on me. *What??? You're a neurosurgeon... Wadda you mean "too extreme"?* He ordered a wheelchair and a convoluted back brace that took fifteen minutes to get on with the help of three people. He told us to go to the university hospital in North Carolina. *Are you serious? We don't know a thing about the area. How's my husband who doesn't drive outta town gonna get me there? I can't go to North Carolina!!!*

I was in shock, and I knew that this was a bad situation. Immediately my mouth opened, and out came the words... "What about Pittsburgh?" I heard the words but couldn't believe that I had said them. The words came out of nowhere. Denny looked at me as if I had ten heads! *Pittsburgh? What?? What the heck do you know about any surgeons in Pittsburgh? Why'd you say that?* I then realized that the angels had put those words in my mouth. That had happened to me other times before when I had said words that surprised me. The angels were literally "covering my back"! All that I knew is that we were familiar with that city only because we were born and raised in the area. *I can't believe that those words flew out of my mouth! I am stunned!*

    This neurosurgeon shook his head up and down as he pulled his phone from the pocket of his white lab jacket. He was searching and scrolling until he found the name of another neurosurgeon. "I studied at a university medical school in Pittsburgh. If you want to go to Pittsburgh, then this is the neurosurgeon that you need to see. He's the best there is." He gave us the name of the Chief of Spinal Deformities, who was well-respected worldwide and a very well-known neurosurgeon in the country. He and his associates worked with the local professional sports teams. We were so grateful that this neurosurgeon knew someone competent who could help me. At the time, we didn't think that Spirit and the Angels were taking charge of my medical care, but they were! *What are the chances? There are no coincidences! Thank you, angels, for intervening for me... big time!*

    Feeling hopeful, the next morning I called the Pittsburgh surgeon's office and got an appointment with the Chief of Spinal Deformities. I prayed that he could fix me as well as he had fixed all the multi-million-dollar-athletes that he had operated on. I realized how grateful I was to get an appointment as I poured myself a cup of decaf coffee with cream. I put the coffee mug on the seat of my walker and rolled outside to sit on our screened-in porch. I thought about how lucky we were to have that North Carolina neurosurgeon point us in the right direction. *This is part of God's plan for me, and I'm sure of that. I know that it was Divine intervention that led us to that surgeon who studied in Pittsburgh and who knew where to send me! Angels, thank you for the words you put into my mouth. I am so blessed and I'm so glad I got an appointment with this neurosurgeon in Pittsburgh. Thank you, God, for Your hand in this new direction I have to take.*

It was then that it occurred to me that we hadn't been in Pittsburgh for at least twenty years or more.

CHAPTER 13

SHANGRI-LA

Sipping my morning coffee, I sat on the screened porch and watched the boats traverse the Intracoastal Waterway and I was happy. Although I was in pain, I was peaceful for once. *We're finally going in the right direction after years of this crap!* In four months, I had an upcoming appointment with the Chief of Spinal Deformities in Pittsburgh. Good vibes were flowing throughout my body. I finally had hope for the first time in the last fifteen or so years. *I can't wait to see this neurosurgeon in Pittsburgh. I pray that he can help me. I haven't been to Pittsburgh for at least twenty years.* When I listened to the words of that last thought, my entire being contracted immediately, and I was filled with horror. *Oh, no...Pittsburgh???*

Wait!! This won't work at all! Hold on a minute... how are we going to drive to Pittsburgh, if we can't drive to North Carolina? Oh, dear sweet Lord! As I sat in my wicker chair, my body became locked in suspended animation, frozen in time and space. My peacefulness evaporated into thin air and my gut bubbled with terror. I had an appointment with a neurosurgeon seven hundred miles away! *How's that gonna happen when we have trouble driving seven miles down the road?* Even if the stars aligned and this neurosurgeon could operate on me, I'd be screwed if I lived down here and had to drive back and forth to Pittsburgh. That just wouldn't work. How are we going to do this? *There's no way on*

Joy Elaine Reed

Earth that we can manage this! Lord, help me! Wadda we gonna do?

"*MOVE TO PITTSBURGH*"... Spirit spoke to me. *Damn - I shouldn't have asked!!! What?? Dear God... NO! Are you kiddin' me?? How the heck can I move all our stuff when I can't even stand up or walk?*

"*YOU MUST MOVE BACK HOME*"... I heard it again, this time it was louder. I sat and gazed through the screens. My mouth hung open, and tears formed in my eyes. *How?* I felt like all the people boarding lifeboats the night the Titanic went down. I was numb! The proverbial rug had just been pulled out from under me. I felt as if I was standing on the gallows with a black hood over my head. My flip-flopping belly started to rumble, and I didn't feel my lungs taking any breaths at all. *How? When? No. No. No! NO! NO!* All my blood had pooled down into my feet and I couldn't think if you paid me. I wanted to die as my catatonic body sat in that black wicker chair. *How the heck is this broken body going to take care of a seven hundred-mile move to a different state? What if my bones are brittle and this Pittsburgh doc can't do the surgery, just like the NC doc couldn't do it?* I never even thought about whether or not I was a candidate for this surgery that I desperately needed. I knew nothing at this point. *Move? From here?*

MOVE???? Moving was never on my agenda. South Carolina was our forever home. We had lived here for the past twenty years. *We got married here. Our cemetery niches are here. Our family of dear friends is here.* How could I move back to the cold and snow? *I'm older now... I gotta have the sunshine. I'll die if I go back to Pittsburgh!* I wanted to stay in this sweet cottage forever and watch the boats flow up and down the Intracoastal Waterway like the hands of a conductor directing a lullaby. Our three-bedroom, single-story cottage that sat at the end of the street across from the boardwalk was my perfect haven. We had a gazebo, a marina, and a lighthouse! *I can't leave here, I just can't! NO!*

I watched the boats float by. Still in shock, I eventually realized the medical necessity of relocating. I made another pot of decaf coffee and I thought about this move all afternoon. My coffee backed up on me... I had so many questions. It never occurred to me that this neurosurgeon would be unable to help me!

My big question was "How?" *Girl, you gotta forget the "how", and just do it. There's no way you can have your back broken in Pittsburgh and travel back and forth while you live in South Carolina. You have no choice but to listen to Spirit. Let go and trust.* Yeah, yeah, easier said than done. But when the Divine intervenes, we have the choice to listen to our calling and move forward or to grab the wheel and make a U-turn. I didn't mess with Spirit. I listened. Spirit always knew better than I. There was always a time and a reason for everything.

I dread telling Denny. I'm between a rock and a hard place. Lord, help me! I thought of a plan. I thought that it would be easier for Denny to accept what I had to say if his belly was full. Physical satisfaction seemed to lighten any blow. That evening for dinner I made chicken with gravy, creamy mashed potatoes, and cut green beans for Denny. It was a valiant effort on my part considering I couldn't stand for more than a few minutes. But, I wanted to fill his stomach so that he was content and happy before I mentioned "the move". Although our dinner came out of a box, a jar, a pouch, and a can, he was satisfied when he finished eating his meal. He knew the pain I endured just to heat up this processed dinner delight, and he was very appreciative of my unflinching effort.

After dinner, Denny washed the dishes, took the garbage to the dumpster, and then came back into the living room to relax and watch TV. *He is such a good man. I hope he understands.* I sat in the wing chair and wished I were anyplace else rather than seated here next to him tonight. I knew he wouldn't want to hear the words I had to say. I sighed and proceeded slowly... "Honey, can we talk?" *I'm walking on thin ice here.* He looked at me as I said, "Babe, you know this back surgery is gonna be extensive. We're talking my whole back here...this isn't just a couple of discs. I really can't have this surgery performed in Pennsylvania while we're living in South Carolina. This is serious business."

"What are you saying?" He turned off the television.

I took a deep breath. "Honey... we need to move to Pittsburgh." When the words left my lips, they felt like a bag of trash that had been left out in the hot summer sun for three days. *It would be easier to tell him that I'm pregnant!* I didn't know what to expect him to say, and I was afraid that he would be upset to the max because we had just moved into our cottage three years earlier after we had sold the big house that we had built when we had first moved to the beach. I sat forward on the seat cushion and looked at him with puppy eyes, thinking that would do the trick. It was a desperate measure.

He let out a loud laugh and shook his head from side to side. "Uh-uh. No. There's no way on Earth that I'm moving back to Pittsburgh." His voice grew stronger. "I didn't come here to move back to PA. I'm happy here. I'm not moving. Do you hear me? I am not moving. Period." A few seconds later he asked, "How do you even know that this surgeon in Pittsburgh can help you? You don't know if he can or if he can't."

I sat quietly with my head down, hoping that he would take pity on me. Tears welled up in my eyes. I was petrified. I realized that I knew nothing about my back surgery but I knew that I had to listen to Spirit. *Please understand!* After a minute I said, "Honey, I don't blame you... I get it... I don't want to move either, but we have no choice." He wasn't biting. I had tried my best but was forced to play a trump card... "Marc will be right there to help us like he always does. We will be able to count on him to drive us to the doctors and the hospital in the city. He's a great Pittsburgh driver. Your daughter and son will be there to help us, too. We'll have our family and great friends back home to support us." He steadily stared at me as I continued. "Honey, we can't be running around from state to state. It's a challenge for us to even drive to the grocery store anymore. We can't be here and drive there. We gotta move."

"I am not moving from here. End of discussion."

I totally understood and agreed with how Denny felt about leaving his South Carolina home. But I knew that I had no other option concerning this matter. I considered his response for a few minutes, and I said, "Then you stay here and I'll move. Honey, we have no choice... Spirit told us to move back home." I was flat-out serious. I never even considered that this neurosurgeon in Pittsburgh might be unable to help me. Hopefully, Denny would follow me when I packed up and moved!

I loved our special cottage since day one and felt that it would be our forever place in the sunshine. The flowers, the gazebo, the boats, and the neighbors who enjoyed a good time and celebrated everything (The sun is out, let's celebrate!!), along with the clubhouse, pool, and boardwalk directly on the Intracoastal Waterway created magic for us every day. My heart ached to think that I had to move from the place that gave me such peace and joy. I remembered what I especially loved in our neighborhood... Irving, the massive thirty-foot cedar tree, and my best buddy, who lived by the lake across the street from the lighthouse. His beautiful energy was so strong and reassuring, and I loved to hug him when we were outside in the breeze. He gave me strength. I remembered the twenty or more mallards that took lazy naps under Irving's shady branches while we sat on the bench next to him. *No... I can't leave here! This place is my Shangri-La.*

When I thought about moving, my stomach did a flip-flop and I wanted to just sit and cry. My back hurt more than ever now and Shangri-La meant nothing to me if I could no longer walk. I had to do what I had to do. We had to move. There was so much work to get done. I prayed for strength to carry out this major move. I needed tons of help. I asked Spirit for guidance and direction. I knew that we were traipsing into unknown territory with the total uncertainty of a possible back surgery looming on our horizon. *Was I even a candidate for surgery?* But I had to trust Spirit. And, I did. *"Trust" is like a tiny seed of DNA that grows into a strong and mighty oak tree that provides considerable strength and hope. Jesus, with all my heart, I trust in You.* Our new moving adventure ended with a question mark instead of a period. At this point, we had no place to go but North. With trust in Spirit, in Jesus, and in a mighty oak tree, we headed to the land of question marks.

In my daily journal, I recorded our incredible journey into the unknown. After he crossed over, Marc asked me to share those entries with you.
There is so much more to tell…

Denny, Marc, and Joy at the beach.

PART THREE:

UNEDITED JOURNAL ENTRIES

Joy Elaine Reed

CHAPTER 14

BOBBY McGEE

SEPTEMBER 26, 2020

We moved into our new apartment in Pennsylvania today. How this all happened is just a blur! My head is still spinning from how it all came together.

Selling the cottage, downsizing for the second time, packing, donating, getting a long-distance moving company, buying all new insurances, paying a relocation specialist to pack bulky items and artwork, avoiding Covid, finding a new place to live in another state, and getting our two cars there - all in three weeks! If I would have considered the magnitude of this move, I would have just sat down in pain on my South Carolina screened-in porch and forgotten all about it. But I didn't have time to even consider this move, everything happened so quickly!

My dear friend from the metaphysical center offered to sell our more valuable items online and split the profits. We had tons of very expensive items that we no longer could use. She needed money to attend seminary, so I told her to keep all the money she got and apply it towards her tuition. (Recently she had been told by another psychic that money was coming her way, although she didn't know how or when. Three days later, I called her to ask for her help!) Spirit already had her lined up to help me and for me to help her! Blows my mind! She also helped me pack boxes of stuff we needed, and she cleaned the house for real estate showings. She was truly a "Godsend". I so appreciated her help and I told her to choose an angel from my angel collection. She chose my favorite angel named "Victory".

My Reiki Master came and helped me wrap and pack some of our crystal stemware. God bless her for her kindness and love. I realize that we can't take a lot of our stuff, but we need a little bit of what we know so that we will be comfortable in our new place.

Denny is in charge of getting boxes from the grocery store. The guy who works there already knows him by name and saves the "good" boxes for him! That's a great help to me, as I'm the one packing everything we own. And, although we are leaving much of what we own behind, we still have a lot of "stuff". The packed boxes fill our living room, master bedroom, and spare bedroom! I can't begin to tell you the physical pain I am experiencing while I do all this packing. God must be giving me strength.

Reverend Richard came and took box after box of food, furniture, and other items for needy people in his parish. Because it is during the Covid pandemic, I had been in a panic, and I had stocked up and amassed four little "convenience stores" in our home, just in case the world would soon be without food. The food costs alone totaled $1,800.00 or more. I watched the Reverend and his helpers lugging huge overfilled cardboard boxes out our front door and I felt stupid for buying all this food. If it hadn't been for the pandemic, I wouldn't have had all that food here. Somehow I felt all this food was what we needed now because I was fearful of our future. I hate being led by fear. But later, I realized that I wasn't hoarding food. There was a reason that I had all this food. I had been used by Spirit to buy that food, not for us, but for those in need. I was being used to help the poor, and it was all good. Spirit continues to amaze me!

Our next-door neighbor was an angel. She packed, cleaned, took care of the house when we moved, returned our cable equipment, and forwarded our mail. She was there when I needed her, and all she wanted in return was to share a bottle of wine with us every night... and, believe me, we all needed it!

I got a price from the moving company I had called and I was ready to book them. Something didn't feel right about them. I got a funny "feeling" that they weren't legit, so I called another company who said that they did only local moves, but to be very careful who I get to move us. Fraudulent moving companies love doing business at the beach. There are almost fifteen untrustworthy bogus movers in our area. The legit local mover told me to call the only reputable company at the beach that does long-distance moving along the coast. I called and left him a message and he called me right back. He told me that he was picking up a load in Connecticut in three weeks, and he didn't want to drive an empty van up there, so he would take our stuff on the trip up! Can you believe this... what are the chances?? He gave me a decent price, too! Wow, I missed a bullet! I can't imagine where our stuff would be now if I had booked the other movers! I just knew Spirit had a hand in this. Then I realized that our entire home had to be packed and we had to be ready to rock and roll outta here in just three weeks!

      Having nowhere to live, I checked out apartments in the area, and found a fifty-five-plus apartment complex that was being newly built about two minutes away from Marc's house! I was so excited, especially because our helper Marc lived so close by, and one of my favorite high school friends was also moving there as soon as the buildings were completed. I called the management company four times. No response and no messages returned. So, I checked the reviews for this company... nothing but bad. Upset people with a ton of gripes. It's a good thing I was unable to contact them. I'm sure Spirit was guiding me away from there, too! Thank you, Spirit! A couple of days later, Denny and I did an internet walk-through of an apartment in a building located in an unfamiliar place close to Pittsburgh. Built in 1955, this apartment had no central air, six kitchen cabinets that were painted white a hundred times, and it was located right next to noisy trains. The rent was insanely high. No way! Spirit was at work again and prodded me to call my best friend Lula who had moved to a new apartment complex in the last year. She loved her new place, and it was in our old stomping grounds. It was about twenty-five minutes away from Marc, but he said he didn't mind the drive. Lula gave me the name of her landlord, and I called immediately. I was told that an apartment would be ready to move into in three weeks, by the middle of September, exactly when we needed it! Wow - blew my mind!!! It was on the ground floor, right off the parking lot. Having no stairs made it handicapped accessible and it had two bedrooms and two baths. What more can we want? I signed the lease and sent the deposit as soon as I could. Thank you, Spirit. Your timing is perfect! Thanks for taking care of us again!

Then I had to figure out how we would get our cars up north because we couldn't make that drive on our own. Denny's son said he would help us, but I had a funny feeling that it wouldn't work out with him and his friend. So I called my cousins who said that we could count on them for help. On September 23rd, we rented a car for them, and my cousins (who don't fly) drove from Pittsburgh down to the beach and stayed overnight with us. They were going to drive us back up North in our own cars. It was so good to see them and spend some time with them. On September 24th, we returned the rental car, and we went to the beach for the last time, although I stayed in the parked car because I was unable to walk over the dunes. That was sad for me, all alone in the parking lot, unable to walk the beach one last time. While I sat there, I "thought" of the pizza joint by the swing bridge. My cousins came back from their walk, got into the car, and told me that everywhere they visit while on vacation, they try out the local pizza. They asked me if I knew of a good pizza place. Yes, I do! We went to the place I had been thinking of, and the pizza was great. This is our last night in our cottage. I miss it already.

On September 25th, the huge moving van came to load up, and we started our drive to Pennsylvania at 9 am. Our cousins were great drivers that came to our rescue! They drove through 7 hours of relentless pouring rain (wrecks were everywhere) at between 70 to 80 miles per hour! It was an awful mess out on the roads. We made it safely to Marc's house in 12 hours! God bless those two gals! We don't know what we would have done without their help...they are such sweet souls and made our trip seem half as long as it was. And they were so patient when we needed to stop a million times for restroom breaks!

We were exhausted. We stayed overnight at Marc's house and drove to our apartment early the next morning, September 26th, while they unloaded the moving van. Marc had to show us where our new home was located, we didn't even know! We just knew that it would fit our needs. We did it! We're here! Somehow I had the strength to keep on keeping on.

Lula, Marc, Denny's son, and our good friends helped us move in. We appreciated all their kindness and caring that day. It made the move go so smoothly. I'm so in pain and exhausted, but we're finally here.

OCTOBER 10, 2020

Marc came back over to our place many times to hang our clocks and big artwork. He emptied boxes and broke them down to fit in the dumpster. He wired up our internet, phone, and TV. He wants to spend more time with his new friend whom he just started dating, and I understand. We take all the help we can get, whenever we can get it. We are so grateful for our family and friends.

OCTOBER 22, 2020

God made my life as it is because He/She knows that I am strong enough and capable enough to handle what comes up. I feel weak but strong at the same time.

I took Denny for a drive so that he can get the lay of the land. I showed him the dentist's office and the mall. Nothing, including the potholes, has changed in twenty years! Then we drove around the community college. I thought that I saw his son stop at the intersection in the bus he was driving. I drove down the road and realized that it was indeed him, so I pulled into a parking space on campus so I could text him and tell him that we have just seen him. *Then Spirit sent us a sign...* Next to where we were parked was a pole with a banner hanging on it. The banner read - YOU BELONG HERE in capital letters. That was the only sign like that hanging on the entire campus. Wow! Spirit is validating our move here. I know this was meant to be. When I think of all the things that worked out the way they were supposed to in our crazy three-week move, I know without a doubt that everything we had gone through to get here was orchestrated by Spirit.

OCTOBER 27, 2020

I went to a pain management doctor to get some shots in my back and hip. I told him about my spinal ablation and that I had to go to the emergency room because the nerves in my back had grown back so suddenly. He told me it couldn't happen that way... it takes a while for the nerves to stop working and it takes a while for them to grow back together again. He said that my pain had nothing to do with my ablation. He doesn't know why I had such immediate extreme pain. What?! It could never happen that way?? Holy smoke! I guess that Spirit really wanted us to move here! Spirit had to use extreme force with me!! I guess that, for me, Spirit has to make things loud and clear and incredibly painful before I listen and get moving!

NOVEMBER 2, 2020

Today is Adam's birthday. Denny and I love him so much and wish that he lived closer to us. He is such a caring guy. He's living in Phoenix and we're in Pittsburgh. We called and sang to him and sent him gifts, but I wish we were together to celebrate all the happy occasions in our lives. Maybe next year. Right now I have no control over anything that's happening in this world of Covid.

NOVEMBER 10, 2020

I talked to Denny outside on the porch this morning. I told him that I get a super-strong "feeling" that we have not moved here only to take care of my back - that there is something else that is the real reason we are here, and it's big. Something big is on the horizon. We are supposed to be here now.

Marc's been cleaning out his place and bringing stuff here that he no longer needs. It's all good stuff. Sweaters, hassocks, sunshine lamps to help with Seasonal Affective Disorder, throws, pillows, and all kinds of nice things. Although he loves his job and his friends where he works, his life is tough. He's seemed not to be cut out to live in this world. He would fit better in a utopian society where every single person is kind, generous, caring, and loving.

NOVEMBER 15, 2020

We have to be careful because Covid has gotten very bad. It's so contagious. Everybody has now either had it or knows somebody who has had it. It's really scary. We don't go out at all (only to our doctors), but when we do we take major precautions. The skin on our hands is peeling from washing and using hand sanitizer so often. People we know are dying. Life will never be the same.

The Earth's energy seems to be changing. I "feel" like we are all being reprogrammed. So many of us have memory loss, no focus, make more mistakes, and have ridiculous thoughts. We are living in chaotic times during this pandemic. It's screwing up everything! Going crazy with the closing on our home being delayed a million times, trying to find new doctors, banks, insurance - and everybody is making mistakes. Someone even wrecked into our car in the parking lot when we were getting our new driver's licenses! Add fixing the car to my long to-do list! It's been such a challenge for me. I'm not used to this madness.

I realize that God gave me a life choice - stay in SC with palm trees and sunshine and water - or - come back here and have the support of family and wonderful friends. I know I have made the right choice, but I miss the beach terribly.

NOVEMBER 17, 2020

I had ordered a rug online that didn't work out. I needed to take it over to the mall to return it at one of the stores there. I called Marc and he said he would take me. He came over with a car full of more stuff to get rid of. He had beautiful jerseys and jackets and all sorts of nice things. Marc had bedspreads and pillows and blankets and towels. Just tons of stuff. It was good that our friend

Lula was at our house at the time because she got to see him again and take whatever she wanted, too. We took what we needed and then he put the stuff we didn't want back in the car. We drove to the mall, and on the way, we passed the animal shelter. He pulled in and was so excited to donate his bedding and towels for the animals. He threw everything in the big bin outside, because nobody could enter the facility due to Covid. He was so happy that he could help the animals...that made his day. Then we drove to the mall and got to the store, and when he opened his trunk, we realized we had forgotten to bring the rug I needed to return!! We laughed and laughed and then drove back to our apartment and I got the rug. Denny thought we were nuts! We drove back to the mall and on the way, Marc asked me what song I wanted to hear. He told me to pick any song. For some reason, "Bobby McGee" came out of my mouth. It was "angel talk" again! We both started singing and having a good time. The words to that song were the story of his life. Then I started crying for no reason. I didn't know why. I felt like I was going to die soon. He held my hand and told me it was all right. I cried and cried, and thought that it was because of my upcoming back surgery (maybe, not sure yet) and that I was old and was going to die. He said everything is okay. He went into the store and returned the rug. Then we walked slowly through another store because I needed some things. I found a robe, a tissue box (he laughed and said he had just thrown away ten of them), and a new rug. He took me home, and then he went home. It was so nice to spend a lot of time with him. I'll never forget us laughing in the parking lot!

NOVEMBER 19, 2020

Marc came over to help me put up Christmas decorations...the "hanging of the greens". When he got here, we just weren't in the mood and I don't know why because we both love Christmas. I can't get into Christmas this year - I can't seem to appreciate this holiday season. This is the first time in my life that I have not been excited about the holidays. Maybe because I hurt so much and don't have the energy. I'm not really sure.

Marc said that he and Adam and his fiancé Brittany wanted to have a nice party for my 70th birthday on Christmas Eve - but we can't because of Covid which is spiking like crazy now. I don't even care. Really. I go to stores and Christmas stuff annoys me - probably because I gave so much of it away when we moved. Whatever. Just not into it this year.

NOVEMBER 20, 2020
Brittany told Adam to call us because she heard that our governor had closed PA and they don't know if they should cancel their plans to come out to visit for Christmas. Damn Covid. We talked and she said they would still try to fly here for the holidays.

I asked Marc to come over today and he could not. I feel like I'm walking on glass when I'm around Marc sometimes. I hate to pin all our needs on him all the time. But, something "feels" weird.

NOVEMBER 21, 2020
My cousins invited us to their home for Thanksgiving, but Marc doesn't want to go. I don't know why but I think he's concerned about Covid. You can't trust who might have Covid now. We'll stay here and have an easy turkey roll dinner. I've invited Denny's kids and Marc's bringing his new friend. Marc and his friend are going to test for Covid before they come over. That's it for us.

NOVEMBER 23, 2020
Today is the anniversary of my dad's mom's passing. I have never thought of Dad's mom since she passed away in 1963! I don't know why I remembered Grandma's passing today - she died so long ago. It was the day after President Kennedy died. I think that I was in 7th grade at that time.

It's been a really emotional time for me now - I'm very weepy. I know I'm supposed to be here now. I have listened to Spirit and have found myself back home. I feel that we must treasure Marc's being here and helping us. Just be so grateful that your son is around.

The governor closed PA. I'm sad because damn Covid is keeping Adam and Brittany in Arizona for Christmas and my birthday. My 70th birthday should be a celebration, but that's not gonna happen this year. This is the first time I've cared about all that is going on around me. We've been staying at home for the past year. One year spent in the house makes people crazy, and much more grateful for family and friends. PA is closed - must be tested before coming here or be in quarantine for 14 days. There's so much to be happy about and also so much chaos and disappointment. I'll miss playing our wild and crazy games. Things are so different now.

Thanksgiving will be different too, and I'm not sure that it'll be good, but I just "saw" my mother giving me two thumbs up. Thanks, Mom.

We finally closed on the sale of our cottage. Marc was our courier and handled the delivery of all the paperwork to the shipping company. It is finished. Spirit has told me to relax - I am wired. Spirit says that now it's over. I can let go. Thank goodness this closing has been completed before Thanksgiving day - something to be super thankful for!

I feel so weird lately. I'm sobbing and feeling just like I did when I walked my border collie, Sally, up to the little cemetery on the hill - it was the first day of the year in 1992. Crying with heartbreak for no reason. Dad got diagnosed with cancer a couple of months later and died at the beginning of the next new year. I guess I got all my crying out early. I don't know. I "feel" the same way now. A big change is coming in my life. I do not know what's coming down the tracks but I have to know that it's part of God's plan for me. It's so hard to accept hurt. I "feel" hurt for no reason. Something is coming up. I am emotionally over the top.

NOVEMBER 26, 2020

Thanksgiving day. Marc brought the new guy he's seeing over for dinner. It was nice and so good to meet him. There were only four of us celebrating the holiday together. We said what we were grateful for, and we all agreed that the love of others made our lives so special. Marc brought his little dog, Abby, and she walked on the blanket in circles the whole night. Poor little thing is blind and brain-damaged, but Marc takes such good care of her. He loved all his animals...his dog Bean lived to be 24 years old - a long time for a big dog. It was a quiet Thanksgiving, very different from others in the past. I missed going to my cousins' house, but don't want to take a chance that we might be exposed to Covid.

Looking forward to my appointment to see the chief of spinal deformities neurosurgeon on December 10th. Lula said she would drive us to the hospital in Pittsburgh. Because of Covid, only one other person is allowed to come in with me, but Lula can't sit all day in the car, so I gotta figure out how to get her into the hospital with me and Denny.

Joy Elaine Reed

CHAPTER 15

SO SURREAL

DECEMBER 3, 2020

    This evening I was shopping online and saw a gorgeous butterfly top. The butterflies were so colorful and there was a mess of them on the bottom of the shirt and they were all flying together up to the shoulders. It was amazing. I wanted it in every color! I tried to buy it but I had trouble with the cart, then my information wouldn't go in, then the promo code wasn't accepted so I said forget about it.

    The local police buzzed our door at 9:30 PM and asked if Joy Reed lived there. Oh, God! Marc must have been in a car accident! He was in a wreck! Oh, Lord! I let the two officers in and they gave me their names and told me to sit down. Oh, God please help me! My head started to buzz. One officer held a small white notepad in his hands. He asked me if I was Marc's mother. He told me that Marc had died. I didn't know what that meant. I listened. It wasn't real to me. I don't know what they are saying. Why are cops in my living room? Denny and I were frozen in our seats. I just looked at the officers and thought it was a nightmare. Marc is dead... what does that mean??? I wanted to tell them that they were wrong. I don't know why you're here. You are totally wrong!

    They handed me a piece of paper with the medical examiner's number and told me to call. I was scared and I couldn't feel any pulse or blood running through my body. I will listen to them because they are policemen. They said the medical examiner was trying to call us all night. The phone did ring all night. I didn't recognize the number that came up on the phone so I ignored all those calls. I didn't ask the officers any questions. I couldn't speak. Denny and I were stunned. I did not feel like Marc had died. Marc did not die. He was just here and now he's not. I felt like it was just news that I was getting, but that nothing really happened to Marc. Nothing that happened tonight was real. The policemen left and I immediately called the medical examiner in the next county and I expected him to say this was all a big mistake. He told me Marc died at around 7:30 PM tonight. He was found on the floor near his work computer. His chair had toppled over with him. His new friend had found him and called 911 but it was too late. The medical examiner told me that since he was 45 years old, he probably died from an aneurysm and died instantly. He said that Marc didn't suffer. The medical examiner was kind. He told me that Marc's cause of death was "pending" until he had the results of the toxicology report. Because of the pandemic, he told me it might take a very long time before the results are back. He asked me some questions. I didn't know what questions to ask him. My brain was not working. He told me not to worry. He said that Marc was there with him and that he was safe. He kept telling me that Marc was safe. Safe? Safe? How could Marc be safe??? He's dead. Everything seems so surreal.

  I called Marc's dad and told him the news but I don't remember talking to him. I called Adam and they were driving home in their car when I told him his brother died, and he almost wrecked and Brittany was screaming to pull over. Dear Lord, I didn't think to tell him that I would call him later when he got home. I didn't know what I was doing. Everything was spinning in my head.

  I didn't know what to do. I felt I had to do something. I wanted to help Marc somehow. I grabbed my rosary and started to pray. I pictured Mother Mary and all the angels guiding Marc to heaven. I couldn't stop crying. I saw Archangel Michael protecting him on his way. Jesus and all the ascended masters met him at the gate with open arms. Gram and Pap were welcoming him, too.

After I had finished praying, I went to the bedroom and remembered his little dog, Abby. The police said that Abby was with Marc's next-door neighbor. Abby became my focus. In the bedroom, I picked up an inspirational book and read where Jesus commanded us to take only one day at a time. I told myself to listen and it was important because that was a COMMAND. I lay on the couch and worried about who would take care of Abby because I knew that Denny and I couldn't do it, and I heard from Spirit... *"TOMORROW'S A NEW DAY... SLEEP NOW."* I was so surprised the next morning when I woke up... I had fallen asleep on the sofa and slept through the entire night!

DECEMBER 4, 2020

In the morning, I got up off the sofa and started to sob. Marc had passed away. He's gone. I walked to the bathroom. Mother Mary had sent me a sign... my silver <u>Miraculous Medal</u> with the image of the Blessed Mother was lying on the carpet in front of my bedroom dresser!!! I was shocked, and I didn't know where it had come from, because it had been in a box in my dresser drawer. But I picked it up and thanked Mother Mary a million times. Blessed Mother Mary was assuring me that Marc had crossed over safely and that she and the angels were with him. I put the medal on the chain I wear around my neck. I will wear it always. I walked into the kitchen and started to clean the sink. It was mindlessness.

Then Marc sent me his first sign... the <u>mercury lamp</u> on the countertop had been on all night and it started blinking. I felt that it was Marc. I asked if it was him and it blinked again to validate that it was him! I asked him if he were here with me and it blinked again! Thank you, God! Thanks, Marc - you made me feel so much better because I truly know that you are where you need to be. Thanks from the bottom of my heart for your letting me know that you are with me here. I need to know that you are with me.

Marc talked to me... I saw <u>him sitting in my recliner</u>... he threw his hands in the air and said, *"I'm free at last!"* I know that he never felt that way when he was here in his body. Then he told me that he was moving in with us. He made me laugh. I am glad and I told him that he doesn't take up much room! He looks happy, relaxed, joyous... comfortable, and content. Seeing him like that made me feel so much better even though I'm bawling my eyes out. I called Denny's daughter and son to tell them that Marc had died. His daughter immediately asked me who was going to take his dog. She said that she would take care of Abby. She adores animals. I said thank you, but that Abby has challenges. She said that we all have challenges and that she's taking Abby. I was so grateful that Spirit handled who would take Marc's dog for us. There was really no need to worry last night. It all worked out.

Denny's niece came and drove me out to Marc's house to get his wallet, keys, etc. Marc's new guy met us there to let us in the house. He is in shock like we all are, and he cried because they had so little time together. I think they've only been together a couple of months. While we stood in Marc's kitchen, we heard a click or a sharp noise - something had moved or dropped. We looked around and saw nothing out of place. Marc had sent us a sign... when I turned to go upstairs I saw Marc's driver's license on the floor a couple of feet behind me, face up with that big smile looking at me. That had fallen from somewhere because that's the noise we all heard. "Marc's here!" I truly felt his energy and he wanted us to know that he was there with us. And, we found Marc's wallet and it's red, just like mine is!

We went upstairs - stuff everywhere. I walked into Marc's office where he had a bookcase partition in the middle of the room. Marc sent the most beautiful sign... I saw his button-down butterfly shirt right in front of me, hanging neatly on a hanger, and it was just exactly like the butterfly jersey I was going to buy online last evening! Marc put it out plainly for me to see. I immediately took it and heard him say, *"Happy Birthday, Mom."* Oh, how wonderful! Oh, Marc, thanks so much! It took my breath away to hear his voice! What a beautiful birthday present from him. Then we gathered his personal stuff and went to the neighbor's to get Abby and we brought her home with us.

Denny's daughter came to our house later to get Abby. She told us that while going to her out-of-state doctor's visit, she was driving down the highway and she remembered a dream that seemed real two nights before Marc died. In her dream, she was with a faceless lady who was seated in a chair. The woman told her to take the "dog with challenges", so she said that she would take the dog and that "we all have challenges". She is convinced that the woman was an angel preparing her to care for Abby. I so believe that! We were so grateful that Abby is getting the best "pet mom" there is!

DECEMBER 5, 2020

My son Adam and his fiancé Brittany, along with Marc's dad and his wife all flew in. It was such a sad reunion. They would only be here for this week so we had to get down to business. We talked about Marc's death and what his funeral plans should be. It was so wild... we talked about what Marc would "want" and his cell phone in the other room would tweet! We talked about which funeral director we would call - the phone tweeted. We talked about cremation - his cell phone tweeted! This went on all night. It was unbelievable! Marc was telling us exactly what he wanted us to do! It was so sad because we couldn't even have a funeral for Marc. At this time, all the funeral homes were closed due to the Covid pandemic. Even two of the local priests had Covid, not that Marc would have wanted a priest. The director of the cemetery told us that on the day of his funeral, we would have to stay outside and that we couldn't use the chapel at the cemetery because of Covid. Only the immediate family could gather around the niche after he was interred. This Covid pandemic changed everyone's life, and it also changed everyone's death. Damn.

I called my cousins to tell them Marc had passed. I had forgotten that I hadn't called anybody but immediate family. I had a lot of calls to make.

Marc's friends started to call me. They told me that they had all visited together at his best friend's house the night he died. There were over 35 people that came. I cringed when I heard this because Covid has been so contagious and spreading... they took a big chance all being together. People are dying from this damn disease. But they had to come together somehow... it was important for them to have each other at this time. They mourned his death and toasted his life. The party ended early the next day. His friends seemed to be crushed. His best friend told me, "If you can count your friends on the fingers of one hand - you are blessed". I was shocked! I was immediately reminded of Dad. That's exactly what my dad used to say all the time! Those words validated for me that Marc was together with Pap wherever they may be! Thanks, Marc, and thanks so much Pap, take good care of him for us. I love you both.

Soon more of Marc's friends called me. They shared how influential and loving Marc had been in their lives. I do wish we could have a wake for Marc...these kids need closure. We need closure, too. *"THEY NEED TO WRITE TO RELEASE THEIR PAIN...TELL THEM TO SEND E-MAILS TO YOU."* Spirit told me that writing would be an emotional release for all his friends since we couldn't have a funeral for Marc. I asked his friends to write me e-mails (because I wanted to help them heal). I got over 55 e-mails that made me feel so wonderful and proud of how sweet and generous my son had been to all during his time on earth, and happy that others were writing to heal. Marc had truly been a blessing to others. Most e-mails told stories of all the kind and sweet things Marc did for everyone, and how he helped them in some way when they didn't even expect it. A couple of e-mails told about how Marc gave people who were gay the courage to come out to their families., and I was sure he helped many more people than just a few to come out. Most e-mails told of fun gatherings and get-togethers and how much laughter they shared doing wild and crazy things with Marc. There were some really funny times his friends spent with him. Some e-mails were so full of love for my son that they made me cry with a smile on my face. They all shared the pain of losing Marc in their lives. His friends who didn't e-mail called me on the phone to share their wonderful love stories about Marc. Other friends planted trees in his memory. Money was donated in his name to save the sea turtles. Everyone has been so good to us - sending cards letters, donations, and wonderful meals for us to have. I especially got comfort from reading the e-mails. These messages and tributes were a catharsis for his friends to write and a blessing for us to read. It didn't make up for the fact that Marc had no formal funeral arrangements, but it was so kind of his friends to share their love for him with our family. Most of the messages I received all said the same things as this message that his former partner posted on social media on the night that Marc crossed over:

'This year hasn't been the greatest. The world lost an amazing person with a heart of gold, but heaven gained another angel. I met Marc 9 years earlier and we were inseparable. Marc showed me so much in our time together and I met so many of my friends through him, friends that have become family to me. Marc was always looking out for the well-being of others and treated me very well, and I will never forget that. Our relationship ended, but my love for him never did. He will always be with me, and I know for a fact, he will make his presence known to me when he is around, and he already has. I wish I could see him again and tell him how much he meant to me, but I suppose it will have to wait til we meet again one day. Until then I will have a beer and a Vegas Bomb for him whenever this pandemic is over. Rest easy, Marc, say hello to our dogs Max and Bean for me. I always have, and I will always love you."

He also e-mailed me a letter that he wrote to Marc:
Marc, I'm not even sure where to begin with this. I wasn't ready for you to leave. I'll start there, but you were never one for careful planning. I remember meeting you for the first time in February. It was snowy and cold... it was exactly how you liked it. We hit it off immediately, our relationship bloomed, and we were inseparable for almost eight years after that. During our time together you taught me so much and showed me a lot of "firsts" in my life. The first time I flew on a plane, the first time I saw the ocean, and my first Pittsburgh Penguins game. Of all the firsts you showed me, most importantly, you showed me how to love. No

matter how mad at me you were, or what petty thing we argued about, you always told me how much you loved me. I will always remember how you put others before yourself anytime you could. You were the first to drop anything that you were doing to help someone in need, myself included. For example, even after we broke up, you insisted that you would be the one to take me to the hospital for minor surgery and took the day off from work to do so. But that's just the kinda person you were, and we were all lucky to have you in our lives. During our time together you also introduced me to some of the greatest people I have ever met. People that are your family, and now I consider them part of mine. You connected me to people that will be my friends for the rest of my life and I will forever be grateful for that.

I wish I could see you one more time, have one more beer, watch one more Pens game, take one more trip to the beach, or give you one last hug. I know deep down that you are aware of how I feel about you. Our relationship ended but my love for you never did. I will miss you Marc, but I know that you will always be with me, and you will drop whatever you're doing to answer me when I need you. I know we'll meet again one day, and I know you'll be waiting to greet me, where ever you are, with open arms. This isn't goodbye. This is "See yinz later". I love you today, yesterday, and always.

CHAPTER 16

AN AWESOME ANGEL

DECEMBER 6, 2020

    I woke up thinking that I have to buy thank-you cards so I can write to all the people who have been so kind to us by sending food, gifts, flowers, cards, donations, and e-mails.

    Denny and I went over to Marc's house again. We were the first ones there and when I unlocked and opened the front door, I had a strange "feeling" that someone was there or had been there. We looked around and went upstairs. There was nobody there and everything looked untouched, but still I "felt" like someone had been there while we were gone.

    The rest of our family all met at Marc's house this morning. Marc took good care of me today…When I got there, I found an unopened pack of <u>thank-you notes</u> on his kitchen table! They weren't there before! Thanks, Marc… you knew what I needed and I'm not surprised. You are amazing. You're still helping everyone even though you are on the other side. You must know how hard this is for me… please keep sending me signs… they do comfort me. Marc sent me another beautiful sign... In his office, hanging on a hanger on his bookshelf divider directly in front of me was a red tee shirt that said, "I'm <u>an awesome angel</u>, take advantage of me". Unbelievable! It wasn't there yesterday! I gasped and started to cry. He is such an angel, for sure. Thanks, Marc… love it! I took it home with me because I knew that he put it there, especially for me!

Marc sent me another sign... I saw a bright <u>red cardinal</u> in front of Marc's house when we were at his front door. I told the rest of the family that I had seen it, and that a cardinal represents a loved one coming back here to tell you that they are doing fine. My family didn't know that and was happy to hear about that.

Adam and Brittany are taking photos of the more expensive items that Marc owned and trying to sell them online. A woman called to ask about the rug cleaner. She told Brittany that she had just lost everything in a house fire. Brittany invited her to come to Marc's and take whatever she wanted... bring a truck and take it all. No charge. I was so thrilled! She came with her neighbor's panel truck a couple of times and took a lot of stuff and furniture and appliances. She also found clothes (probably new with tags and expensive) for her son and husband. She told us that now she can have Christmas gifts for them and she was so happy. Her mother gave her an <u>angel for the top of her Christmas tree</u> and she said she named it "Marc" because she said that he is truly an angel who helped her after her fire! (Remember what the red tee-shirt says!!). It's so wonderful that Marc is helping people after he is gone from this earth. I believe that - because that's the way Marc is. He is and will always be a fountain of kindness.

Marc's dad and his wife, along with Adam, Brittany, and Denny worked hard today, going through mail, etc. It's very hard to do when you're crying. I did the best I could. We all spent a long time looking for Marc's important papers... it was all too much for me, so Denny and I left the house later that afternoon and headed back home. The rest of the family stayed and worked the rest of the day. I don't know what we would do without their help. Thank you, family, and Infinite Power of Love!

DECEMBER 7, 2020

I thought about the red angel tee shirt that Marc "gave" me when I walked into his office and saw it hanging right in front of me. We were in our kitchen and I asked Denny if that tee could perhaps be my Christmas present from Marc since he told me that the butterfly shirt was my birthday present from him. Could that be possible? Denny looked at the clock on the stove and told me to look, too. The time on the clock read 12:25!!! I couldn't believe it! Marc was validating that his red angel tee is my Christmas gift this year. Wow! Oh, honey, thank you so much. That is so sweet and special. I love you. I love how you send me messages!!!

Today I stayed home and called the medical examiner, funeral director, and cemetery supervisor. I'm trying to get Marc's burial plans coordinated since there can be no funeral. I have so many questions. It was a hard job, but it felt good being away from Marc's home for a while. I did get answers to my questions.

Brittany asked me if there was anything that I wanted her to bring me from Marc's house. I asked Brittany to bring Marc's jewelry here and told her exactly where to find all of it. There was a box of chains hanging on the wall next to his bed, and there were a couple of wooden boxes on his dresser filled with jewelry. He had boxes of nice stuff, and jewelry that I had bought him that had crystals and energy healing stones. When she came here later for dinner, she brought a shoebox with a few pieces of costume jewelry, but I knew Marc had better stuff and there was a lot more. She didn't see any box on the wall or the two wooden boxes on his dresser. I told her that I had a funny "feeling" that someone had been in his house. I had just given Marc the window security cameras that I couldn't use at our place, so Brittany said that she and Adam would check the security cameras when they return to his house tomorrow.

The family is doing a great job of cleaning out the house and getting rid of stuff. They are working like superheroes. Usually, organizations come for free to take the stuff that you donate. But nobody's picking up stuff now due to Covid. We had to pay a couple of guys almost $3,000 to come to get his stuff and haul it away. It was all good stuff... they're probably going to sell it.

DECEMBER 8, 2020

I drove out by myself to Marc's house to get packages that were delivered to him that his next-door neighbor kindly picked up. Denny needed this day to stay home, nap, and regroup. I walked into Marc's house and Adam and Brittany were standing in the kitchen and seemed shocked. They told me that they checked the front and back cameras and the front one had fallen off the window, but the back camera worked. Instead of taking a video outside, it reflected off the back patio door and back into the house where a light was on in the living room. The kids saw Marc come into the living room, walk around, sit on the couch and look around. They were sure that it was Marc! They tried to pull the video back up so they could show me... but it was gone! Marc must have come to relax in the home that he loved! I'm not quite sure they knew what to think, but they said it was Marc in the living room! I don't doubt that! They said he was just looking around at all he left there. And the fact that they couldn't pull the video up again to show me was a validation that it was a sign from Marc and it was meant just for them to see.

We went upstairs to Marc's bedroom and Adam found all of Marc's jewelry that I had said was there! There it was hanging on the wall and in boxes on his dresser. We called Brittany upstairs to Marc's bedroom and Brittany was shocked. She said that what we had found of Marc's was definitely not there yesterday! I know that Marc made it disappear so that they would have to check the cameras so he could show himself to them! I truly believe that he hid all his jewelry so that they would check those security cameras. That was so kind of you, Marc, but you scared them to death! I don't think they're skeptics anymore!

When we walked into Marc's office, there was a small guardian angel plaque on top of the frame of the closet door facing Marc's desk where he passed away. That angel was directly behind the desk chair that he was sitting in! Marc was telling me that the angels were with him when he passed! That sign made me feel so happy. And, it's weird because Marc had no other angels anywhere else in his house!

I saw a picture of Denny in a clip frame. He was sitting on a boat in Capri, wearing a jacket Marc had sent him. Marc kept that photo on top of his television cabinet. I got the photo down and behind Denny's picture was a laminated inspirational card that I was always sending to him. It was a text from the Bible, Ecclesiastes - and it said, "there is a time to be born and a time to die". Marc was telling me that this was his time to die. I heard him say to me, *"We all have a time for everything and this was my time to leave you. If I didn't die the way I did, I would have died some other way. I might have gotten hit by a bus, or something else would have taken me. When it's your time to go - you go. This was my time."* I started to sob. That gave me so much comfort to find that card behind Denny's photo and to hear him tell me that it was his time. He made me truly understand that there was nothing anybody could do to change things or the way he died. It had been written and was carried out the way it was supposed to be. Thanks, Marc. I love you. I understand why you are not here with us now. But, honey, I miss you so much.

    The kids loaded my car with stuff that I had given Marc that I didn't want to leave behind. When I was pulling out of my parking space, Adam came running up the steps to stop me. Adam was all excited and he pointed out a huge red cardinal singing in the tree in front of Marc's house. He was the biggest, bright red cardinal I had ever seen! Adam was so thrilled and he knew that Marc was here with us and he wanted me to know. That's so cool. I am happy that Adam is aware of signs from Marc.

    I got a headache before I left Marc's house. I never get headaches. I was dizzy and felt sick. Although the kids didn't want me to drive - I drove home. I felt like it was a psychic attack. I tried to clear the energy, but it just got worse. I felt faint and I couldn't breathe- the pain in my head was pounding and lasted for about 5 minutes as I kept driving. I heard, *"Mom, this is how I died"*. Then the headache went away. This has happened to me before. I am an empath and I have felt someone else's heart attack and another person's stroke. Not fun. Very scary. I am so glad that Marc let me know because now I know that he didn't suffer long, if at all. I think that this sign gave me so much comfort today because I heard Marc's voice talk to me. I love to hear his voice, and I know that he's right there with me! I am so very grateful for the many blessings and his signs.

DECEMBER 9, 2020

Today is our family funeral service for Marc at the cemetery. I don't know how to conduct a funeral. It's strange. Somehow I made it through this day without breaking down! I know that if I had not been connected to Spirit I would have never gotten through this week. In the morning I went into our spare room and looked through my crystals so I could put some in Marc's penthouse with him... that's what we call his burial niche because it's high up on the top row. And it's funny because when I told his best friend that we got a niche for Marc on the very top row, she said that it was Marc's "penthouse" - That's the very word she used, that same word I had used about one hour before she said it! So I feel that Marc knew about his penthouse, and approved! I found a miraculous medal with the image of Blessed Mother Mary with my stones so I put it in with the crystals in the black velvet bag that will be in with Marc when he's interred. I put in his dogs' collars and a picture of Abby with his stones and the rainbow maker he had given me as a gift a long time ago. I keep praying to Jesus and Mary to keep Marc safe and hold him tight. Finding the medal was Mother Mary reassuring me that he is good. Thank you, Mary.

Marc is sending wonderful signs to help us through this week... I started to write my letter to Marc that I was going to read at the cemetery at our little family gathering. I wrote "You Did It"... he truly did accomplish his life's purpose. My letter was long and filled with love. I sobbed while writing it. As soon as I finished, Denny's watch started ringing for about three minutes. I know that Marc was thanking me for my letter to him.

I went to the kitchen drawer to get the scissors and the "What do you see" business card with the word "Jesus" written in the background was on top of the scissors! I haven't seen that card in forever. I don't even know where it came from. I know without a doubt that Jesus and Marc are together and it's all good. Thank you, Jesus. I trust in you, Jesus is holding me and Marc in the palms of His hands. We can rest now.

Marc's dad and his wife came to the house and I was sharing about all the times that Marc has come to me and all the signs he has sent me - and then I looked at the clock and the time was 11:11. Marc validated that he has been sending these signs to us. That's a mighty powerful angel number saying "It's all good"! That made me feel so calm and I "knew" deep in my soul that everything was good. It still doesn't take away the grief, but it helps a little bit. I don't know how long I'll have to go through missing Marc, probably forever, but his signs are such a comfort to me when I'm sad. But I know that he's here with us. Thank you, Marc. I love you so much.

We gathered together at our house before the six of us went up to the cemetery at about noon. We all wore orange jackets, hats, coats, and sweaters that we took from Marc's place. We were the only people there. It was the coldest day of the year and the wind was biting. At the cemetery, we walked towards Marc's niche, and Adam said that we looked like a bunch of deer hunters all wearing orange! That's funny and so true. We had to laugh. It was good for me to laugh when I wanted to scream. Thanks, Adam, for your sweet observation! I opened our "service" with a prayer, thanking the Lord for being merciful when Marc dropped his body so suddenly and we thanked Mary and the angels and Archangel Michael for taking Marc to the other side safely. We thanked Jesus and the ascended masters for meeting him, and we thanked God for giving us Marc to have with us for 45 years. I read my tribute letter to him, telling him that I was so happy that he had accomplished all he was sent to earth to do. He is a good man who loved others and blessed them. I am so proud to be his mom. Everyone else shared their tributes. Then I read the meditation from a beloved book I own - it said exactly what I had read to Marc... blessed are those who follow God's will. Marc did just that... he brightened peoples' lives. Marc did what he was sent here to do and then he went back home. We finished our service with more prayers. The kids noticed 3 little scarecrows on the grave in front of Marc's penthouse and they were all facing Marc's niche. We called them "Marc's Posse" because they were all wearing orange clothes!

The sun came out during the time of our service and then it got cloudy again after we were finished! The back of Marc's remembrance card says "I'd like the tears of those who grieve to dry before the sun"! Marc had sent the sun to dry our tears. He validated that he attended our funeral service! I knew that he would be there. How cool is that? Marc, we're glad you were there with us. We were freezing cold, but you were not!!! Love you.

We came back home and Adam shared that Marc made him cry at the restaurant last night. During their dinner, Marc sent Adam a sign...at the restaurant they played Marc's and Adam's favorite song when they were little. Adam said he felt Marc with him and he choked up. He said he was embarrassed because there he was, this big guy crying at the table. He misses Marc. We all do. Crying is normal, and although we don't like it, we must do it. Tears are a necessary release.

Britt and Adam went to the top of the hill on Mount Washington to take pictures of the city - there was a rainbow that appeared in the sky even though yesterday was a bright, sunny day with no rain!

More signs from Marc...while we were all eating dinner here tonight, the phone rang at 7 PM... the word "Highmark" came up on the phone screen..."Hi, Marc"! Seriously? Marc ate dinner with us tonight! He was with us all day and I know that. Boy, he's trying to make us happy and tell us that what we did for him was all good. He appreciates the funeral we gave him, as pitiful as it was. It's good knowing that he was with us all day.

I "feel" that everyone's content with getting through the week however we had to do it. It was the toughest week of all of our lives. We are all sad that Marc's gone but we're happy that he's free. I am truly happy for him. I heard Marc's voice again...he told me, "*I can't be hurt anymore!*" OMG! Does anyone know just how much at peace I feel to hear him say that?!!!! That's the one thing I needed to hear. Thanks, Marc. I truly believe that you are in a better place and that you are safe.

One of Marc's neighbors whom he loves called to tell me a story about a plant stand that Marc had given her. She told Marc to take it back when her plant died in the fall, but Marc told her to keep it for when she gets another plant. They love each other. Recently, Marc came to reassure her... One day this week, after Marc died, she looked on her porch and saw a little bird hopping around the stand. She never gets birds on her back porch. She said it was so little that it looked like a leaf blowing around. She looked closely as it jumped up onto the stand. She was so surprised to see <u>a little robin</u>. When she told me the story, she said that she felt that it was Marc saying hello to her, because loved ones often appear to us like birds. I told her that it IS Marc because it's so unusual - robins don't come here until the spring! And my sign from my dad is always a robin! Marc's with Dad and he's telling us all that he is okay. Thanks, Marc!

DECEMBER 10, 2020

Marc came to my husband in the middle of the night...Denny told me he got up at 3 A.M. and the TV was on. The <u>entire screen was orange</u>! Everything... people, words, script, background. All orange! Denny hasn't taken Marc's messages seriously, but now he sees! He is a skeptic no more. Marc wanted to reassure Den that he is doing fine where he is.

More signs... I have crystals on my windows and Marc's been sending me <u>rainbows on cloudy days</u>! On my desk and dresser, on our bed, and the wildest... I put laundry detergent in the cup and it formed a film over the top. I watched the film turn into rainbows. I asked Marc if this was a sign from him, and the rainbows spun around! Then I asked if he was okay... and the bubble popped! He's sending me <u>moving rainbows</u>! He knows how much joy rainbows bring me. Thanks, Marc. I love you so much and I'm convinced that you are in such a wonderful place of peace, that everybody there is celebrating you coming home to them, and that you are probably at one big celebration party. Welcome home. I wouldn't want to have you back here with me... I could never be that selfish. But, I know that you are here with me while you are there where you belong. I'm so glad you can now be at more than one place at a time and I am thrilled for you and love you dearly! I miss you, but that's because I'm your mom and I have big love for you.

DECEMBER 11, 2020

I woke up in the middle of the night and a sitcom was on TV. It was a storyline about how much <u>the brothers love each other</u>. Marc sent that message to me so I would know that he truly loves his brother Adam. How beautiful is that? I laughed because I never watch that TV show! But, I knew why it was on my TV at that time!!

Marc gave me another gift…I went to my closet to get a notebook out to keep track of our transactions for Marc. There were 5 blue ones and one <u>bright orange one</u>! I grabbed the orange one, of course! LOL. "Of Course" is what Marc always said and we had that printed on the window of Marc's penthouse! Marc made me laugh. I know that these messages from Marc are subtle, but I am so on the same channel with him.

All the family left to go home today. They had worked so hard this week and we were so grateful for their help. Denny and I couldn't have made it through this week alone. We all have taken the items we wanted from Marc's place, this stuff he held dear to him has now become very dear to us. I took an unwashed jersey that was in his laundry basket and that smelled like him. Oh, how I cry every time I smell his scent. It's like he's right here with me. I am so glad I took that jersey home with me. I hold it often and it brings me peace.

I remembered this past Thanksgiving with Marc. That was the last time we were together. We took turns around the table saying what we were thankful for - and we were all thankful for each other. It was the nicest Thanksgiving I can ever remember. A big box of mix-and-eat stuffing and love. Love. Love. Love. It will always be my most wonderful memory - the last time we were with Marc. I was with Marc because I was here in Pittsburgh. God put me here to be with Marc before he dropped his body! That's why all those recent events led me to be here, to spend quality time with Marc before he passed. It was so nice to be able to give him a big hug and kiss when he left our house on Thanksgiving Day. If I still lived at the beach, his death would have been too terrible for me to endure. This way was best and he "knew" it. We were together before he died. I wonder if Marc knew he was checking out and worked with Spirit to get us here? I really don't know. I guess that it was all Spirit's doing... and Spirit has perfect timing. Thanks, Spirit, for blessing me and bringing us here to have time with Marc.

One of Marc's friends called me and is having a really hard time missing him. Anytime those two got together it usually spelled trouble. Once when they went to a burger joint together, an armed robber came in carrying a gun and had everybody lie on the floor! Marc said they were really scared for their lives. (Archangel Michael was working overtime again that day!) There was always some kind of excitement when they got together. I remember when those two went on a shopping trip and bought baby chicks that she wanted to raise in her backyard... and they gave Marc a pin that said, "I just bought a chick today" or something like that! He had texted me a picture of him wearing it! LOL. I talked to her and told her that Marc will always be here with us and she asked me to please send her Reiki, which is divine healing energy. Reiki is great for calming and centering. Being a Reiki Master Teacher - I sent Reiki out to her and all Marc's friends. When I called all of Marc's friends to my mind, I pictured them - and I saw hundreds of thousands of friends gathered at the Mall in Washington, DC! Marc's love had a ripple effect - moving out in ever bigger circles. He was a healer. He was a Light Worker and he accomplished his divine purpose. He did it! Marc, I am so happy that you did what you were sent here to do.

I am filled with such hope when I see the signs that Marc sends to all of us here on Earth. I know he wants us to know that he is safe and happy. Those signs bring love and hope to my heart and I know "it's all good" when I get a sign. Thanks, Marc. Please keep them coming.

Marc with a "C", Brittany, and Adam

CHAPTER 17

FOOTPRINTS IN THE SNOW

DECEMBER 14, 2020

Marc's friend called me and shared a story with me. Marc came to him... He dreamed that he and his son were sitting on the ground in a park throwing stones into a river. He saw a man walk towards him. He recognized him. It was Marc. They sat down together and threw stones in the river for a while. Marc told him that it was good to see him again and told him to take care. Then Marc stood up and walked away! How beautiful it was that <u>Marc came to him</u> after he had passed. Wow! I wish I would dream of Marc. I would love that.

Lula and many of Marc's friends have planted trees in his memory. There's a place to do that online on his obituary page. That's so kind of them. He had so many friends. I don't think he knew the impact he had on people's lives when he was here on Earth.

DECEMBER 16, 2020

My metaphysical friends from the beach held a Celebration of Life for Marc at their chapel. I watched it on my computer and went through five boxes of tissues. The music they played was all my favorite songs. Wonderful words of comfort were shared. It was so beautiful. I called my friend who had held Marc's service. She told me that "Marc will help me in ways that he could not while he was here". That was very kind of her to hold this service for him. I know that he was with me when we watched it on the computer. I just felt him next to me.

DECEMBER 18, 2020

Lula came over and gave me a lovely birthday card and a generous gift. When I went to hang my card up with all my other cards, I heard Marc tell me, *"MA, LOOK AT THE BIRDS"*. There were two birds on the front of the card and they were both orange!! When did you ever see <u>orange birds </u>on a card? Lula didn't plan for that! I love you, Marc. You're too much!

Marc sent another sign to start my day...This morning at 6 a.m. I saw a commercial on TV and the <u>dog's name was Frank</u>! That's Pap's name! Marc, you know that these subtle signs you send me bring me so much comfort... I know that Dad is with you and I am thrilled. Please keep sending me messages and signs. "Frank" is meaningful to me, so I know it's a sign.

My mom and dad's old neighbor called us tonight to tell us how sorry she is that Marc has passed, and she said to me, <u>"Marc is with Frank"</u>!!! Whoa! Dad is validating what I heard this morning on TV!

DECEMBER 23, 2020

We visited Marc at his penthouse. Denny wore a Steeler Santa hat and I wore a big sparkly Christmas tree hat. We're trying anything to lift our spirits. Marc must have liked seeing us looking crazy because, on our way home from the cemetery, a truck pulled out in front of our car and went as slow as molasses. Marc told me to look at the back of the truck... the name of the business was <u>"McGee"</u>!! That's wild! Reminds me of the song we sang together before he crossed over.

One of Marc's business associates told me how much she adored Marc. She said he was always happy. She and her husband lost their son when he passed away last Christmas and they understand what it's like for us. She lovingly sent me an inspirational book that gives me hope every morning when I read it. That was so sweet of her. Hope and peace…doesn't get any better than that! I know that they are going through the same hurt that we are, and I also know that Marc and her son are probably best friends now on the other side! They were both born on the same day!

DECEMBER 24, 2020
    I had a very quiet birthday. Happy 7-0. I wore my butterfly shirt today, Marc's birthday gift to me. I don't know how to say how I feel today.

DECEMBER 25, 2020
    When I woke up today, there were 8 inches of snow on the ground!! Marc wished me a Merry Christmas…when I went out on the porch, there was snow on the porch floor. I have a little ceramic bird sitting on the bottom of our railing that reminds me of the birds that perched on our front porch window when Denny had his bypass surgery…they were there to tell me it's all good! Anyhow, under this bird on the railing were little bird tracks going from directly under that bird and towards our door!! It was a track of <u>bird prints in the snow</u>! The tracks came from a ceramic bird! It was so surprising and so beautiful. I was thrilled to see tracks only under the bird and nowhere else on the porch! I knew that Marc was with us and that made me happy. Merry Christmas to you, Marc. We really miss you.

    Almost every Christmas card we've received this year has a <u>red cardinal</u> on the front! Cardinals are such a beautiful psychic sign, Reminds me of loved ones coming to tell us they're good. It is amazing! Unbelievable!!!

    I have learned a lesson through this time of moving and losing. I have learned to put things in motion (do what I need to do) and then let it all go and let Spirit take care of the results. Marc crossed over before me because I needed to learn the lesson of releasing and letting go of everything. When you lose a child, nothing matters anymore. Nothing matters but love.

DECEMBER 26, 2020

It snowed all through the night and through this morning. Marc sent us another sign...the ceramic bird on the front porch left new and different tracks in the new snow! That's Marc, I know it is. He's reassuring us that he is well and happy and for us to move on. It's all good and we will be safe! It's so funny to see bird tracks right under that ceramic bird that can't move! Nobody would believe it, but I took pictures! Too much!

DECEMBER 29, 2020

Marc surprised us this morning...The awesome heart painting that I bought for Denny when he had bypass surgery started to make noise today. It's hanging on the wall in the dining room and it's making noise! What!? It clicked like it was sending Morse Code. It was loud enough for me to hear while I was sitting at the table. It was so funny! I know it was Marc talking to us! Thanks, honey, good morning to you! Love you.

Yesterday morning the time on the coffee pot was 322 and I noticed that number because it is important to me and Denny. This morning I saw 322 on the coffee pot again! Thanks, Marc, I love you. I love it when you repeat numbers for us to see.

DECEMBER 30, 2020

The coffee pot read 322 again today, the third time in a row. Marc's sending me numbers. He's telling us that he is with us in our new apartment.

Cindy and Pete sent me another beautiful card to cheer me up. They are so sweet. It cheered me, then I cried and cried, missing Marc. Marc came to me...I felt a cold chill and I felt Marc wrap his arms around me from behind. And he gave me the biggest hug! It felt so good! Good morning, honey, and thanks so much! I love you.

I just hope that the signs Marc is sending us are signs I can use to help me help others. I hope they reoccur because then I will know exactly what they mean.

I was watching a cartoon sitcom on TV tonight that I had never seen before in my life. The couple was arguing about their anniversary date. The woman told the man that the date is September 3!!!!! That's <u>Marc's birthday</u>! They were standing in front of a cemetery! A time to be born, and a time to die... Marc's telling us that it's all good! Thanks, Marc.

JANUARY 3, 2021

I was thinking about how wonderful it would be to be where Marc is in Spirit and I asked Marc if it was awesome where he is...Marc answered me immediately...the <u>grandfather clock struck 12</u>. That's the number for perfection and cosmic order! Marc told me that it's mind-boggling there! He said he is free to be who he is!! That's beautiful! I am so happy for him.

Today Marc sent me hope. I had called about a bill I received and I talked to the customer service rep who was yet another mother who had lost her child 2 years ago and she understands "Mom Brain"...having a mind that's sometimes like a sieve. She told me to take life second by second. I seem to belong to a huge "Moms Helping Moms Club". It's so good to know that I have the <u>support of strangers</u>! But we're all in this together. I am a magnet for grieving parents and that's great. We all help each other.

JANUARY 8, 2021

I realize that Denny, Marc, Adam, Britt, Denny's daughter and son, and I have had amazing "love experiences of the soul". We love each other in the same intense way that God loves us. Love that knows no bounds and lifts us and touches our souls so deeply that it's hard to believe that it is so. How blessed I am to have these soulmates to share "crazy, unbelievable, everlasting love". Love that's amazing and beautiful and eternal. It's almost as if we share each other's souls. Thank you, Lord, for such a beautiful and wondrous gift. I am so grateful.

JANUARY 9, 2021
Marc's saying good morning to me...I woke up at 5 A.M. and the TV was on and the only words I heard were..."Marc Alan". It was an ad for a plumbing company whose name was Marc Alan, but spelled differently! Good morning angel!

JANUARY 10, 2021
Marc's here!... Denny's heart painting vibrated again today! It sounded like Marc was tapping out a code again. Lula was here to hear it, thank goodness someone else heard this or people would think I'm crazy! What do I care? I know they already do! I'm crazy but harmless! LOL
I thought about all the like-minded friends I miss in South Carolina, and I heard Spirit tell me... *"YOU HAVE LEARNED ALL YOU COULD WITH YOUR SOUTHERN FRIENDS AND NOW IT'S TIME TO MOVE ON SO THAT YOU CAN GROW SPIRITUALLY."* That's why I'm back in PA. Seems like such an unlikely place for intuitive spiritual growth - but I'm going with the flow. I can't wait to see how this all unfolds!

JANUARY 13, 2021
I saw a rainbow orb that was very very bright, almost too bright to look at, in my rearview mirror while I was driving across the bridge today. I was floored. This is a sign of "unconditional love". This is powerful! It is rare and very special to see. Marc spoke to me...
"Mom, I want you to know that I have crossed over just like you are crossing over the river on this bridge now. I am with Archangel Michael. He is protecting me and I am safe."
Wow!!! That was Archangel Michael's Orb...and it was wonderful to see and feel his mighty presence! This is something I never will forget. Although I have a book of my photos filled with angel orb energy, I have never seen such a blinding angel orb as this.

Archangel Michael is a powerful protector whom I call on every day for protection. Thank you, Archangel Michael, for keeping Marc with you and keeping him safe. I love you both with all my heart and soul! Please continue to watch over Marc and continue to protect and bless us all. You are the great protector. Thank you. Thank you. Thank you.

JANUARY 15, 2021

I had a "knowing". God showed me the meaning of suffering. Dad suffered from cancer. Mom suffered from emphysema, broken bones, and physical pain. Marc suffered from migraines, rejection, discrimination, and hatred. Yet during their suffering, they were still able to love. Oddly enough, there is goodness in suffering. Here's the important aspect and the reason for the suffering... "suffering" gives us the opportunity to help those who suffer. This, in turn, gives blessings to us as caregivers and those people who pray for the suffering. Additionally, It allows those who are left behind to see the very real blessing of our loved ones "crossing over" to the light of unconditional love and peace and joy.!! How beautiful is the knowledge that our loved ones are released from their suffering!? What a wonderful feeling to know that they are free! Their release gives us great comfort and joy. Marc said that he is free now and I believe him. Their pain and suffering ultimately make it easier for us to accept them leaving the pain behind and birthing into Spirit. Their suffering brings us peace. It's important to suffer to help others heal. Suffering has meaning.

JANUARY 17, 2021

I did a reading for a client yesterday and I "felt" that she had a baby who had crossed over. She said that she did. Another one!! I am a magnet for grieving parents! Today I asked Spirit, "What is the meaning of all the mothers and fathers who have lost children that are now in my life? Am I supposed to help them? Spirit answered, "*I SENT THEM TO HELP YOU*!!!" I was floored! I know this is a blessing for both me and them. Thank you, Spirit.

JANUARY 22, 2021

I heard a noise by the front door. I thought Denny was in the bathroom and the noise was coming through the wall, but Denny was in bed sleeping. I investigated. There was <u>a tapping on the wall behind my photo of a rainbow</u>! This is the second time that's happened. I know it's Marc. He loves rainbows as much as I do! Then I heard Marc say, *"Mom, I know that a part of you died when I left this Earth. That part of you is with me always and we will never be apart or alone."* Wow! What he said made me cry.

Footprints in the snow.

CHAPTER 18

SENDING BIG LOVE

FEBRUARY 3, 2021

It's been exactly two months since Marc dropped his body and returned home. I am still raw. My emotions go up and down. Marc's passing is still fresh. A couple of days ago I was talking to my friend Andie, and I was thinking that I wanted her to give me a reading. Two seconds later she asked me if I wanted a reading!!!! Yes, I do.

Today I had my reading with three psychic mediums... Andie, Donna, and Elizabeth are all my friends. The only information they carried into the reading is that they know me and they know that my son died. They always meditate and call souls in before the reading, and they have their information in their notebooks and do not confer with the others before the reading.

Andie started the video reading... she saw a core of deep sorrow in me... a bird that flies away and would always return but then flew off to the golden sun (my psychic sign for Jesus "Golden Son"!) and didn't come back. She said that she feels like I'm here now but also in Spirit at the same time, that I go back and forth (Marc sees me between both worlds and he is right, now I don't know where I belong!) She mentioned something about soup (it was the last meal Marc brought over for us!!) There's a weight pulling me down (my heart is very heavy). Marc sees me staring out the window (yes - I have been going to the balcony door a million times a day and looking out - it's mindless but something to do - don't know what I'm looking for!!!). That I have a sense of silence and I'm waiting for that sound (Marc's right - I don't know what I'm searching for but everything to me seems so quiet). He calls you "Ma". (yep, that's Marc). She referenced seeing "feet" or comparing the size of feet. (I didn't get that reference at first, but then I remembered...Oh, how funny, Marc took a graduation picture leaning against a ladder with his leg up on the ladder, and all his friends at the pub teased him and struck the same pose and sent all their pictures to Marc! When we looked at that pic together a couple of weeks before he died, I told him that his feet looked huge and that they looked like boats! Marc's reminding me of what I said. Marc's here and he's so funny!!!). She said that this soul was a dreamer and very sensitive, and trusted people too much. (Yes, indeed). He worked hard. She saw the words "Harmony" and "Victory" and said he is now liberated. She saw a man come forward, a grandfather who is serious and dependable (Pap) and he lent Marc energy to come forward. Another man came in and felt like another grandfather... he was very blunt.. he is also with Marc (could be Marc's other grandfather?). I see a row of trees and a house (Pap and Gram's house). Many headaches (Marc had migraine syndrome). Yellow all around him - he went down immediately (he died immediately, surrounded by the golden light of Jesus). Both grandfathers were there with him as soon as it happened. She saw him swimming... Marc said, "Mom was always there to hold me up." (He was a swimmer and I always did my best to support him). He told me to go outside at night and look at the velvet sky and stars and we'll be together. I see a picture of you two together. (There's a sweet picture of me and him together when he was about five, and it's next to my bed and I look at it all the time). Denny's little dog who has passed is like his little brother and is with him all the time and won't let him alone... (this little black poodle was abused by a woman with mental illness and only trusted guys so this makes sense, just wrong gender). He feels freedom. (Marc told me he was free.). He made his own choices and it's not my fault... Marc says, "Get over it, Ma". Lights blinking. (He makes our lamps blink.) He's a prankster. He and Denny's dog MeMe will be there to meet me when I come. He hasn't left me - he loves me. Look in his dishwasher and stove, there may be something in there. He came to her surrounded by a brilliant yellow/golden light (yellow denotes heightened expression, happiness, freedom, and the golden light of Jesus. The word "halo" means "golden" and is the symbol for perfection. Marc is in a perfect state.)

Then Elizabeth said that he was young when he died. (He was 45.). Long hugs - he loved to hug (yes, his hugs were amazing!!!). He said cutely "I'm sorry - I can't believe it was so fast" (talking about the way he died.) He said that I got parts of him that nobody else got. (absolutely!!). People only got a fraction of him. He showed her a small caesar salad and the cartoon car with a rack of brontosaurus ribs on the top (oh, how funny - he hated veggies - he was a meat lover!). She asked him to put something in her hand and he gave her a rose and a rosary and she said that no soul has ever given her two items (I immediately prayed the rosary the night he passed and the rose is my sign for unconditional love - Marc was thanking me for praying for him! I know that it mattered that I prayed). No pain. Light-headed. Peace and calm. Stop obsessing about the way he died (I do think about it often and I know that it does no good.) You see tall shadows, it's him, don't be skeptical, he is bugging you at home in the shadows (I see tall shadows here all the time). She said she could feel his profound love for me. She said it's "Big Love" (I can't believe I'm hearing this… on every single thank you card I wrote after Marc died, I ended by saying, "Sending Big Love"!!!). He said that he left immediately, "I didn't have time to shut the door." (That's such a blessing. He didn't know what was happening to him.)

Andie then heard him say, "That damn dog is stuck to me like glue!" (so funny - that's how that dog was with Denny!). He told me to "Smell the shirt" (he knows that I took his shirt from the laundry basket and every time I smell it my heart fills with love and good memories).

Donna showed me her notebook and she had written on the top... "Meet your mark" (she had no idea of his name!). He told her, "This is how it happened, Ma." (That's him). The skinny kid grows fast (yes). She saw something about feet! (validates Andie's vision about feet). She saw a figure-eight (my psychic symbol for eternity - we will always be together). Cooking, and recipes (Marc had and treasured all of Gram's recipes!). Piano music (Marc took piano lessons). Rainy days are very very sad for me - don't let the gloom empower you - clear it and raise your vibration. Marc said, "I gave you a sunshine lamp Ma, you gotta plug it in and turn it on!" (Yep). Pull in your guides and angels and use them. Release your throat chakra - "Dismiss the jury, Ma, you're allowed to grieve."(thanks so much, he's right). She talked about a grief seminar (I've been meeting with a group of grieving parents and I have also registered for a soul journey workshop). Then Donna shared a message from Hannah, a group of higher beings whom she channels... "Circles - I never get out of them - clouds, people, pain, and drama circles - gray stone labyrinth - amethyst - female walks with me - man walks with me and we walk the labyrinth - a Super Moon lights the path - a powerful woman is my guide through the labyrinth - there's a bench in the middle - a young man is there on the bench and has the "little shit dog" - he says there's no shit in heaven - he leaves you messages in numbers." (That's so like Marc saying that!!! And he leaves me numbers everywhere!!)

I felt that all the gals were spot on with the messages they gave me, and Hannah was spot on with telling me about the circles of pain throughout my life, and that I have the support of my deceased parents and the Blessed Mother Mary. I have amethyst geodes in every room in our house. The Super Moon signifies feminine power - I have to be powerful in this gray labyrinth, but Marc is there and he does leave me messages in numbers, all the time. It's so funny that Denny's dog won't let him alone! She is still so needy! I feel like our personalities don't change when we cross over and that people can still identify our souls.

What a wonderful reading. I am so grateful that Marc came through loud and clear. That was powerful for me, knowing that

Marc is here with us always. Knowing that he is not gone from us. He truly lives on. Feeling his presence in this reading. I am so grateful that he came forward to give me comfort. I know that takes a lot of energy for souls to come through to loved ones here. It's all good and even though my heart is breaking I feel strong. Nothing can erase love, but I miss my baby. I started to cry and I heard Marc say to me, *"It's okay to cry. I've been a mother and I understand."*

MARCH 1, 2021

I've been grieving hard these last few days. Today Marc showed me 333 (my number sign for being surrounded and loved by all the ascended masters and Jesus) on the coffee pot, and the time 10:10 (a powerful angel number that signifies change and growth and trust for a wonderful new future ahead). Thank you, Marc, your number signs comfort me.

MARCH 2, 2021

Thinking about my upcoming surgery which had to be pushed back until the end of May. Hoping that I'm doing the right thing because this is one big deal! Spirit and Marc keep telling me that it's all good.

I saw 10:10 (a powerful angel number that also signifies enlightenment and spiritual awakening in life, and 12:12 a powerful sign that I am fulfilling my life's purpose). Also, Denny's phone dialed itself and made a call to Marc! And a photo of me and Marc popped up on my friend's iPad and she texted me the photo! Lots of signs today. Nice!

MARCH 3, 2021

Saw 10:10 and 4:44 (a wonderful angel number that lets you know that you are surrounded and loved by many guardian angels and that you are safe). Thanks, Marc and angels, for your wonderful signs to me. Donna was right, Marc you're sending me tons of numbers and I know that it's all good. I'll go forward and trust. I have hope for the future.

On my kitchen counter this morning I found a folded yellow post-it note with stamps that had not been canceled inside, and on the front of the post-it note in <u>Marc's handwriting</u>, it said... "A little something for the Denster! Marc always called Denny the "Denster"! And Denny loved to collect stamps that had not been canceled. For me to find this note with stamps on my kitchen counter was so beyond amazing. I know that it came from Marc, but I don't know how he put it on my counter! I know you are here and all is well. Thanks, honey. You're too much!

MARCH 10, 2021
The medical examiner's office called today to tell me Marc's official cause of death. It was ruled accidental. He died from a fentanyl overdose. I asked him what fentanyl was because I didn't know. He said it was a drug that dealers put in other drugs to cut the cost but it is deadly. He said Marc died immediately from pain pills and fentanyl. I felt like I was living his death all over again for the second time. NO! NO! This isn't fair! Oh, Lord, what more can I take? I knew that Marc took pain pills. Anger, shame, guilt, rage, helplessness, embarrassment, self-judgment, and self-condemnation - it all came flooding over me. What? Why? How?. Was I oblivious? I wondered why I didn't take him to the rehab center but he told me he knew what he was doing because he had taken pain pills all his life. He never acted as if he was on anything. This is so sad. I feel that I could have helped him, but I did nothing. Even though I talked to counselors and rehab centers, he insisted he was fine. Oh, dear Lord, forgive me. This is so sad. I called Adam and told him the news and that I felt like I was a horrible mother. After we hung up, Brittany called me back to set the record straight. We all tried to help but Marc refused. They wanted to get him out of the scene and invited him to stay with them in Arizona. I had stopped giving him money. We all tried. This is a nightmare for me. I am so angry at Marc. I shouted at him and told him how angry I was. Then I started to pray. I prayed and prayed and finally, I heard, *"MARC WAS HURTING. THE SYSTEM GOT HIM HOOKED AND HE COULDN'T DO ANYTHING ABOUT IT.* I had

drawn my head into my shell because acting like a turtle was normal for me. I was tired of dealing with Marc's situation, he seemed to need help all his life. Damn it all. He was hurting - I felt helpless. Whatever. We both did the best we could at the time. I cannot judge him. I cannot judge anything. I just know that Mary, the angels, and Jesus brought him into heaven. He's there and he's safe with Archangel Michael. He is loved unconditionally. I can be mad at the pills and the dealers, but I have to remember my love for him and his pain and hurt. Nobody can judge pain.

MARCH 18, 2021

I leave the TV on all night because it brings me comfort and I woke up in the middle of the night and a sitcom was on TV. A woman's son was a cross-dresser and he had passed away. She could not <u>deal with the shame</u> she felt. Her friend told this mom that her son had an amazing capacity to love and that's the only thing she should remember about him. That's exactly what I needed to hear and I know that my waking up in the middle of the night and watching this show was a blessing from Spirit. Marc was a man with an amazing capacity to love. Period.

I talked with my friend Donna today. I shared that Marc died from an overdose but she already knew. All the gals that gave me the reading knew, but they didn't tell me because they knew I would find out when the time was right. She told me that Marc couldn't come to me for help because he was too ashamed and now I feel HIS shame and it's four times worse than my shame. She said that my shame goes way back to childhood and that being a parent of a gay guy just piled more shame on me. (Her son is gay, so she understands.) She said that Marc's shame was worse. And I'm feeling all that pain - Marc's AND mine and it is too much to bear. She reminded me that Spirit gave me 2 months to work through this before my surgery. That Marc's time for dropping his body was perfect - thank God it happened before my surgery. She was so good to me and her words were so comforting. I know why I was led to share my feelings with her. She said that I have to put light and love around us both. I know that God is holding our hands. I know that this surgery will set a lot of things "straight" (literally) with me. Spirit brought us back here for a reason. Only good lies before me.

    I told Marc that I was sorry that the life he chose brought him so much pain...but there's a reason for the experience of living a gay life and the shame that brought you pain. I don't know why it was part of your life's path, but I'm happy that I gave you your life and that God sent you to me. He knew how special you were and he blessed me with you. I will always love you and I want you to know that it's okay. We both did the best we could with what we had. But the love we shared was so good and true and I know that love is all there is. We were 2 people with such deep levels of shame and nobody could help - so there was no reason to believe that we could help each other. We are truly birds of a feather. I couldn't help you and you couldn't help me. I forgive you and I forgive myself. We did nothing wrong but to live lives filled with shame. There's nothing to forgive! Donna helped me to see the big picture. We're both living in shame - but, not you, not now! Your shame is over and you want me to let go of my shame now and live free... for the very first time. And I will do just that. No more shame. NO MORE SHAME. THE SHAME IS GONE. I will go forward with my head held high and know that I am proud to be your mother and part of Almighty God's universal energy. And I will look up at the stars every night and know that we are together. I miss you, honey. Donna said she just sent her son a text and sent "little rainbows" to him and that's not what he needed but that's the only "mothering" that she could do. I get it and did the same thing. Trying to make everybody feel good and make the world a better place. That was a tall order! Hey, honey, both of us tried our best. It's over for you and I am so happy. And I know that you want it to be over for me now. And so it shall be. There is so much more for me in this life. I am going forward with the knowledge that although the world may say "shame on me" or "shame on Marc", we are no longer carrying that shame. Let them say what they will about me if they want to judge. Who gives a care? Really? Their judgment of me means nothing. I will not hold onto shame any longer, because you and I are beings of Love and you can't get any better than that. Marc, I love you. I am so happy that you are free and that nobody can hurt you anymore. Thanks to you and everyone on the other side for helping me to drop my shame and move forward knowing that I have nothing to be ashamed of anymore. Thanks, Spirit for letting me see the light.

Later that day I was searching for a shamrock emoji so I typed in "shamrock" and nothing came up. The next time I went to use my phone I saw the word "shame" in the search bar. This is Marc telling me to let go of the shame. It isn't mine to have. God does not judge - God loves.

I now have a feeling of peace. I feel the light of Spirit. When I let go of the shame of Marc's being gay and overdosing, I will then be able to move forward. I feel truly connected to that light that we all possess (Marc, Gram, and Pap, too) which makes us one with God and each other. We are never alone. We are always in the light of love.

I realize that there was nothing that I did or said that could change Marc. I realize that it's not our job to change people because, like my friend Zara always told me, we don't know the journey they are on and what karma they are trying to work out. What do we know? I can't change anyone but myself. With God's help, Marc was the only one who could change Marc, if a change was what he needed. "Free will" always overrides the whole system

MARCH 27, 2021

Denny and I received the most wonderful and beautiful gift today that was delivered to our house. Adam and Brittany sent us a special quilt that they had custom-made for us. It was made from squares cut from the front of Marc's tee shirts!!! They were all the tees that we remembered Marc wearing. Oh, what an awesome surprise! Holding that quilt feels like holding Marc in my arms. It was so kind and generous for Adam and Brittany to understand the importance of sending Marc's tees sewn into a quilt. Those tees were Marc's life story!!! Adam and Brittany must have collected them when they were here during Marc's funeral week. Wow, that's something!! No wonder we love them so much! They are such an awesome couple. I am so glad that they found each other! God bless them both, as much and more than they have blessed us!!

CHAPTER 19

SWOOPS

APRIL 20, 2021

I've been noticing that Marc's energy shows up as a <u>swoop of opaque light</u> across the photos that Adam and Brittany are sending me. He's letting us know that he is with us. His energy is not round like an angel orb. It looks like one big paintbrush stroke across the photo. We have seen a swoop in a ton of photos we've been taking! Some swoops are white and some are all the colors of a rainbow! It's so nice to know that Marc is with us and wants to enjoy life with us although he's on the other side. He wants to be with us and have fun with us! Thanks for sending us your swoops! We've come to know "the swoop" as the face of Marc!

I have my "Marc quilt" on the sofa and the last couple of nights there were <u>rainbows of light</u> on it and when I picked it up, it felt like <u>it was wet</u>, but it was not. Denny also says he feels wetness down the left side of his back, and I felt his back and there's no wetness there. It was the weirdest feeling. It actually felt wet. Must be Marc! These signs are so unreal and wild, and I love them.

APRIL 21, 2021

Marc's on a roll today. He sending a ton of signs. The first thing I saw today was an <u>orange butterfly</u> on a TV ad. Then I looked through the guide on the TV and saw a show "<u>McGee</u>" which is the song we sang together before Marc died ("Bobby McGee"), and the name I gave to our peace lily that my dear friend sent us as a sympathy gift.

I have a small orange rubber squeeze animal with a light inside and today when I touched it up it <u>immediately started blinking</u>! It never does that! You gotta squeeze that guy hard to make him blink!

Then at lunch, there was <u>a bright rainbow</u> on the wall by the grandfather clock. Hiya, Marc! Also, today <u>Marc's college</u> was on the news when some guy from the area donated 4 million dollars. That college is a small private college and is never on the news! So many references for Marc and all these signs tell me that Marc is fine and more alive now than he ever has been. I know he's here, and I can feel his energy around me.

I also feel like he is busy working on a project on the other side. It feels like he's working with animals and with St. Francis of Assisi. I know that he is in that place of peace that surpasses all understanding - just like I felt many times before. He's in that beautiful and loving place that you want to stay in forever. Where nothing matters but love. NOTHING can take away that peace. I'm so glad that Marc is there now and doesn't have to be here to help me with whatever will come about with my upcoming back surgery in May. Although I know he'll be with me all the way - helping me in ways I would have never expected. And I'm grateful that I did not add to his stressful life by needing him to help me with my back surgery now that we're living here.

APRIL 23, 2021

Marc's <u>playing with our toilet paper</u>. LOL. I put a new roll on the holder and grabbed some sheets and the roll fell on the floor and rolled across the room towards the door. I picked it up and put it back on the holder. Then I went to the sink to wash my hands, and after that, when I turned around, the toilet paper was all rolled out and in front of the door again! Thanks for making me laugh, Cark! You know I needed it badly! I see you still have your wonderful sense of fun and humor. I love it!

APRIL 24, 2021

I talked to Andie. She said that she was so happy that Marc came through in their reading. Since she had never known Marc or had seen a picture of him, I sent her his picture and she said that was exactly how she saw him! She felt like she knew him. Isn't that beautiful!? They are truly connected.

I was cleaning my desk when I found the folder with all the emails that Marc's friends had sent to me after he crossed over and I started to read them all. The first one that I looked at was written by Marc's friend the night he died. He sent it to me and all Marc's friends the very next day:

Remembering Marc

I wasn't blessed to know Marc as well as some. But in the relatively brief time I got to know him, I learned that Marc was a very spiritual guy with a heart as wide and deep as the ocean. He would almost always greet me with a "Hiya Pal" and a heartfelt embrace, often with an "I love you" thrown in.

Marc had a great capacity to love and, consequentially, to be wounded, too. I ached for him at times. But he was a wonderful friend and I always enjoyed my time with him. Most of which was spent at our beloved neighborhood pub. Perhaps this isn't the time to share this with all of you. His passing is still so fresh... so sudden and utterly devastating. But the best way for me to deal with my feelings and emotions is to remember the good times with him. And I thought sharing these moments might help you, too. Hopefully, Marc would like that.

Who's Gonna Drive You Home?

One night Marc and I were at the pub just before closing time. He'd had a few too many as we all have from time to time and was in no condition to drive. He asked me to drive him home in his car. I said, "Sure." After all, he lived what... about 100 yards away. How difficult would it be?

Very... I was soon to learn. When I sat in the driver's seat I could barely reach the steering wheel, let alone the gas pedal. It

Joy Elaine Reed

should be noted that Marc was about 6'3" and I'm around 5'9". Having never driven anything resembling a late-model vehicle, I asked Marc for his keys and he said I didn't need them. Then he instructed me to push a button on the dashboard near the steering wheel to start the engine. Oh.... Next, I asked him how to move the seat up, since the pedals and I were barely in the same zip code. He told me to press a bar on the side of the seat. Well, I fumbled around and found buttons, but no bar. The seat reclined up, the seat reclined back. I swear to God it turned sideways. But I didn't get any closer to the pedals. By this time we were both laughing so hard we were in tears. Somehow, I managed to get him home without damage to life, limb, or property. It was probably my favorite all-time Marc moment.

In the Drink

It's common knowledge that I'm about the last person on the face of the earth with a flip phone. Marc, who worked for a technology company and was ultra-tech savvy, hated my phone and was always trying to get me to upgrade. Whenever we would text, I'd sprinkle in a few "bloops" and "bleeps" to mimic the sound it made when I typed. My phone can't translate animated emoticons... they display as boxes. After a while, Marc would say, "I box you pal" instead of "I love you."

Well, one night down at the gym I dropped my phone in the drink. Yes... the toilet. Fortunately, it was fresh commode water (if there is such a thing) and I gingerly fished it out and dried it off. So phone-dense am I, it didn't even occur to me to open it up and dry off the battery and inner workings. At first, to my amazement, my phone seemed to be okay. But after a while, it started to display psychedelic patterns on the screen like it was on a bad acid trip and began to heat up. Thinking it might blow up, I wisely (?) turned it off. Arriving at the pub, I plopped down in the seat beside Marc and glumly explained to him and our bartender what had happened. "Let me see it," Marc said, rolling his eyes while snatching the phone from my hand. Within seconds he'd opened it up, removed the battery and memory card, and was drying *everything off with a napkin. Then he instructed the bartender to get some dry rice from the kitchen and a plastic bag. "Put your phone in the rice and leave it overnight," he instructed. "It might work in the morning." Then he generously offered to let me choose from about a half dozen old phones he had lying around his place. As silly as it sounds, I have a sentimental attachment to my phone, So... I did as Marc said. The next morning, I sprang from my bed, put my phone back together... and much to my astonishment (and his chagrin) ... it worked. In fact, it's still working to this day! I owe it all to Marc, even though he never stopped trying to get me to upgrade, ("I can put you in an upgraded phone for around $300," he said the last time I saw him). He's responsible for the fact that I still have it.*

There were a lot more moments with Marc. Some are comical, like the time he broke my glasses while giving me a hug. Many deeper and more touching. Like the night he told me to value myself. Along the way, he helped change my thinking about a lot of things and got me to see things differently. And maybe that's what it's all about. Friends helping each other and maybe sanding off each other's rough spots and making their lives better. God bless you, buddy. It was my pleasure and privilege to be your "pal". And I know you're in a better place... a place of peace and rest and beauty.

I laughed and cried at the same time when I read through the tons of emails his friends sent to us. Maybe it was a good thing that we couldn't have a "proper" funeral with visitations at the funeral home for Marc because the emails that his friends sent to me right after he had passed far outweighed anything that they would have said to us at the funeral home. We probably would have just had small talk and I would have heard how sorry his friends were, and many other words that said the same thing differently. All the same stuff everybody says at funerals because they don't know what to say and they feel obligated to say something. I know... I've been there. But these emails are genuine and meaningful and sweet and hysterical. They are a wonderful tribute to Marc. They show me how much Marc was loved by others because of who he was and the love he showed to them. These emails are priceless and precious and I shall keep them always. Everyone that sent me an email got a thank you card from me. I signed them all with, "Sending Big Love". It took me weeks to finish them all, but I did it because I was so appreciative. Marc had so many friends and they had so many stories. These emails are so comforting and they have eased my pain. Maybe everyone should send an email tribute to their friend's family after their loved ones cross over. It beats the heck out of saying "I'm so sorry" for lack of better words.

APRIL 26, 2021
Today I talked with a friend and told her that sometimes the pain of Marc's death is too much for me. She said that when I struggle with something there are two things I must do - I have to change and I have to accept. I don't have to approve or like what I must accept. Something in me is triggering what I don't like about this situation. She told me, "Marc did not choose his life to make waves in your life." Oh, when she said that it immediately hit home. She was right. God doesn't want you to have bad feelings about a family member who has passed. Just love Marc for who he is. I need to release my anger with this whole situation.

I'm mad at the world. I am mad that life sucks. And, I am mad at Marc. I was mad because he lied and wouldn't accept my help. Then my friend asked me, "Could anybody tell you what to do when you were Marc's age.?" (No.). She ask me, "Did you ever lie to the people who loved you?" (Yes.) "Why did you lie?" (Because I didn't want to hurt them.) "There you go!" I am also mad at myself. She told me that I can't fix anybody. Marc lived his life and made his choices, and what he did was none of my business. I get it. These are all things that I know. I guess this is part of the grieving process. Everything I want to let go of will keep coming back so that I can work on it and release it. It'll take time, and it'll keep coming back over and over again. And that's okay. Grief sucks. But it's insane to carry anger for something I cannot change. I will get through this with God's help and Marc's messages and signs. I will claim my power and move on in peace, one day at a time. This too shall pass.

Joy Elaine Reed

CHAPTER 20

POISON

APRIL 30, 2021

I spent the morning wondering about addictions and wondering how God and life work. I was trying to sort out things in my head. Marc came to me and said,

"Mom, know that God's always on our side. And it's not because we are people who do good - it's because people ARE good. We are a part of God and God is love, so we are all good. Life and its challenges are what you face when you choose to come into the world at birth. All challenges are lessons to learn from and move on. In hard times, some people become victims and allow the challenges of life to keep them stuck with their wheels spinning. Who wants such misery? Those are people that give up and let life beat up on them and never change or move forward. Other people learn their lessons, break free of the bad situation, and push themselves out of defeat. You gotta push yourself to move forward, it's not going to happen without effort on your part. Sometimes you just have to grow up."

"You gotta work at being happy because you're here to be happy and make other people happy. How much mental and emotional work did you do before you could experience happiness? And, once you started to feel that joy, how many other happy people moved into your life, to bring you constant happiness? That's what you call being blessed. You

know it takes a lot of energy and guts to move forward and I'm happy for you. Each of us has a life path, and if we tough it out, we move forward. You have a purpose for being. You come to Earth for two reasons - to raise your vibration so that you can then raise others' vibrations, and also to become happy, joyous, and free. And you become free when you do what God wants you to do - make the right choices that will bring you closer to Him/Her. But know that this takes work on your part. No victims will ever be happy. Only heroes are happy. Become a hero."

I wanted to know why so many people feel trapped and worthless. "So why are so many people not happy, joyous, and free?" I asked a pointed question.

"Fear. Fear is what takes away your joy and separates you from a relationship with God. People think that the opposite of love is hate but they are wrong. The opposite of love is fear. You are either living in love or living in fear. Trauma causes fear. Many people are living a life in which trauma plays its part in the center of the theater stage. Ma, you were traumatized when I dropped my body and returned home. Everybody has experienced some kind of trauma. Many humans have endured traumatic situations and because of that, they are living in fear. They are fearful because they have been mentally, physically, or emotionally abused... they have experienced being beaten, stalked, molested, raped, bullied, accosted, silenced, abandoned, attacked, ridiculed, mugged, threatened, or harmed in some other way. They may have experienced a sudden health challenge. Anything that causes stress is trauma and you always become on high alert for the ball to drop again. You call it Post Traumatic Stress Disorder and it makes people continuously anxious. You live in fear that the future will bring a repeat performance of stress to deal with. Because of the continuing trauma, you turn to addictions. And any compulsive repeated actions become addictions.

Compulsive shopping, hoarding, overworking cleaning, eating, people-pleasing, drugging, drinking, gambling, and so on, all make you feel good because when you are into your addiction, you forget about your fear. Addictions make you feel that you have a moment of peace in a traumatic world. It's one of the ways to comfort yourself and protect yourself against what you fear."

"How do you protect yourself? How do you release your fear? Are there other ways besides turning to addiction?" The answers to these questions were important to me.

"Nobody's ever found peace at the bottom of a bourbon bottle. The best way to let go of your fear is the toughest. You must stop your addictive behavior entirely and trust in something much more powerful than you to give you peace. Try God. Everyone has thought about God, because God is love, and love is all there is. Even if you don't believe that God exists, you gotta believe that there's a power greater than yourself. The Universe didn't evolve because you made it so. Trust and turn to God as you understand Him/Her or turn to whatever you feel is your higher power. Then release your fears to God and turn your will over to God. You gotta lose yourself in love. Without fear, you will no longer need your addictions. Let God take your fear away one day at a time. God is a benevolent power that you can trust and will grant you comfort as you release all the fear that you have been so tightly clutching. GOD WILL KEEP YOU SAFE SO THAT YOU NO LONGER FEAR. Choose the path that brings you closer to God and helps you become happy, joyous, and free."

"It's not easy because we all have such big egos. Egos are not our friends… we are not all there is, and that's okay. The true path to peace lies in trusting a higher power. But so many people avoid an intimate relationship with God because they are afraid that "God will get them" for being such a bad person. Not true at all. Some beliefs may be

based on religion. Religion isn't Spirit. Your relationship with God is based in your heart. No matter what your religion, just know that you are loved and will be loved forever. God is like a giant eight-gazillion-piece jigsaw puzzle and you are blessed to be one little piece of God. God is good and so are you. God is love and love is not capable of judgment or revenge. PEOPLE ARE NOT "BAD", THEY JUST MAKE ERRORS IN JUDGMENT AND WRONG CHOICES. "Forgive us our trespasses" should read, "Forgive us our errors". This is important. Everyone can become closer to God if they choose. But you have to drop your egos first. It's never been all about you. BECOME HUMBLE."

"Addictive behaviors are another way people use to relieve stress and feel safe. This is not the way of peace. People have a desperate need to move forward without fear. People that feel the need for safety must let go of their fear in one way or another. To turn your will and life over to God is truly a release. To take on addictions is the bull-headed, egotistical two-year-old "I'll do it myself" approach. Addictions and compulsions are sneaky in how they make you feel safe. You feel less fear if you wash your hands 60 times a day to rid yourself of "dirt", or smoke 2 packs of cigarettes a day "to calm you", or overeat to the point of vomiting, or starve yourself because you feel that you don't deserve to live, or take drugs to stop the pain both physically and emotionally, or drink a bottle of vodka and pass out. The result of all addictions is to relieve pain in some way."

"Addictions become dangerous because they are excessive behaviors repeated frequently. Eating one piece of cake, smoking one cigarette, taking a pain pill for a headache, gambling in a casino for ten minutes, having one martini - some people can handle that. Other people feel the need to frequently repeat these behaviors to feel safe. Some say it is a disease and I do agree. These people seem to have a trigger in their brain that is set off by the one pain pill or drink or whatever it may be. It's very easy for them to fall *into the "I need more now" zone. That's what happened to you so long ago when you were addicted to food, and it's what happened to me, too, Mom. I had an addiction to painkillers. The doctors freely gave them to me all my life and my body got used to them and they made me feel safe and gave me what I thought was peace. I was afraid to give them up. I didn't know where to turn because I needed them. Addiction is a terrible beast"*

Telepathically, I told him how I felt. "I wish that you had been addicted to something other than drugs. They killed you!"

"All addictions kill, Mom. It's not just drugs. Being morbidly obese will kill you. Drinking to excess will about melt your liver. Look at Gram! She was a two-pack-a-day smoker and she smoked cigarettes even while on oxygen!"

I defended my mother. "Yes, but she didn't do drugs."

"Ma, what was the cause of death written on her death certificate?"

I clearly remember because I was shocked when I first read it. "Cigarette Smoking" was Gram's cause of death written on the top of her death certificate. "She died from cigarette smoking which caused emphysema and nobody could tell her to stop smoking."

"Any way you slice it, she was an addict, Ma. Smoking cigarettes made her feel less vulnerable. That is what all addictions do - help you to feel less vulnerable and more in control."

"Most people seem to think that some addictions are "okay" and some are "bad" which is not the case. All addictions change the life-force energy of your body and make you unbalanced physically, mentally, socially, emotionally, and spiritually. Using drugs is no different from using alcohol, compulsive people-pleasing, buying fifty purses, or being a control freak. Is there an order here? Drugs = very bad, Booze = kinda bad, and people-pleasing and control freak and compulsive buying = okay. Look how crazy that is! And, Ma, I know that you are afraid that people

will judge me or judge you. Who gives a care what people say, anyway? All people judge, and all people have opinions. That's their stuff to own, not yours. Don't take it personally! Judgment and opinions about you belong to someone else."

I felt extreme sorrow. I told him the truth. "I hate what your addiction did to you."

"I'm so sorry you feel that way because I love you, Mom. But while I had an addiction, I was always able to function and I did not want to quit using. I made choices that were not wise. But, know that I had no intention to die, Ma. When it happened so suddenly, I was more in shock than you were. My death was immediate and I was stunned as I quickly left my body. You may think it was all my fault but it was not. My death was carried out by another's hand. Someone who didn't even know me poisoned me and intended for me to die and knew that I would die. My death was a homicide. I WAS MURDERED, MOM. I took the pain pills but I did not commit suicide. I was unaware of the poison that I was taking. The people who did this callously put fentanyl in those pills just like someone who puts razor blades in kids' Halloween candy. Knowing that it will kill, they do it anyway, and they don't care. That's how I died, Ma. I was poisoned. It was murder. It's alarming and the number of fentanyl overdose deaths is increasing daily. Any dealers responsible for the fentanyl death of another person can now be charged with murder. This is how it should be, but it won't bring back me or others who were poisoned and killed. It's a deliberate act and a travesty that should not be happening."

Hearing this made me crazy angry. My son was murdered. His life was taken from him. What could I do? "Can I find out who did this to you?"

"The police failed to treat my death as a crime scene because they thought I died from an aneurysm. This was a crime scene but it has been compromised. But those

murderers know who they are and they know what they did, although they did not know me. You can ask questions, Mom, but you won't get any answers. The deed has been done. And what is sad is that so many people are dying from fentanyl overdoses and there are no answers. People are not aware of the poison they are taking. One kilogram of fentanyl has the potential to kill 500,000 people. That's enough drugs to kill every person in Kansas City, Missouri, just from one kilogram. That's crazy. This drug additive is potent...and without lab testing, it's impossible to know if there's fentanyl in a pill. Most, unfortunately, almost half of the pills tested for fentanyl contained the lethal dose of 2 mg. There's a lot of killing going on and it's getting worse every day. Did you know that the dealers are now marketing fentanyl pills that look just like everyday pain reliever pills? It's everywhere and it's out of control. Where will this killer drug be found next? People are too trusting and think they are invincible, but they are not."

I couldn't believe how horrible this situation is and that I didn't know anything about this until Marc passed. "I'm in shock. What can we do to stop this?"

"Can you stop drug trafficking? Can you stop the dealers? No, you can't. This is as bad as the Covid pandemic killing people all around the world. The sad part is that the Covid pandemic will slow down but the fentanyl deaths will escalate because they are increasing every day."

I thought maybe we could take a different direction. "What about stopping the addictions? Wouldn't that solve the problem?"

"You can go there, but remember that you can't fix anybody. You can tell others the risks (which I'm sure that they already know) but they think that "it can't happen to me". Nobody ever expects to die. I didn't. You can drag a person you love to rehab and repeat that performance enough to lose your house, car, possessions, and sometimes the *people you love most in your life, but still, your loved one may die from an overdose. You have met so many people that have been through that because they thought they could fix somebody. Remember, you can't fix anybody. Ever. Each one of us is on our own life path. You don't know what I need and why, and I don't know what you need and why. We're given our lives, our journeys on Earth are necessary to work through some old karma and raise our vibration. No one truly knows what anybody else needs. MOM, YOU COULD NOT HELP ME. No one could. I made my choices and did what I needed to do when I was on Earth. It was my time to leave, and I tried my best to leave in a way that was gentle for you. I could never hurt anybody."*

"Oh, Lord, honey, I hate to think about how you crossed over but I think I understand. The way you died was a blessing in so many ways and I am grateful every day. I know it sounds strange to be thankful for the way someone you love leaves their body, but it could have always been worse. I wasn't there with you when it happened and I didn't find your body and I'm grateful for that. I know I could never have handled that. Thanks, I appreciate your concern and love for me."

"Most souls leave the bodies in a way that's the easiest for those who love them and are still here. Mom, please know that nothing I did, no choices that I made lessened my love for you. Our love is eternal."

"We have free will and no one can force their will on another. Not you, not me, not the angels, and not God. No one can mess with your free will. Although people try their hardest, you can't fix anybody unless they are willing and ask for help. So, since everyone has free will, you have no reason to feel guilt or shame about my dying. It was my life and my will. I made my choices. My life was not your journey to make. We each have our own needs and fears. WE CAN'T HELP OTHERS UNLESS THEY ARE WILLING. If it isn't yours, it

isn't yours to take on. **NOBODY SHOULD FEEL GUILTY FOR THE CHOICES THAT OTHERS MAKE."**

His last sentence was like a heavy, warm blanket being wrapped around me and it brought me comfort. I understood everything that he was telling me, and I was grateful that we spoke to each other today. I am not responsible for the choices anyone makes in his or her life. Live and let live. I did try to help him but it wasn't to be. The words he spoke made me understand things a lot better. I didn't like it, but I had to accept it. Acceptance is the key. I know I'll work through this somehow. "Thanks, Marc, for clearing up a lot of stuff for me. There's a lot here that I didn't consider. I truly appreciate you talking with me today… anything you can tell me is truly comforting after I think about it. I need to process this information and I will ask the angels to help me. I need to keep letting go of pain, shame, anger, and guilt, and your conversation with me today did help in many ways. It will take time to join my head with my heart. I know that time is on my side and, as I feel my feelings, my grief will become less stinging. Just know that I love you dearly, and I miss your hugs more than you will ever know. I'm sending big love your way, Cark, now and forever!"

Joy Elaine Reed

CHAPTER 21

CHRYSALIS

MAY 2, 2021

Today in a parking lot Lula and I parked next to a car with a small, tiered-crystal chandelier hanging from the rearview mirror. It was adorable and it threw <u>rainbows all over</u> the inside of the car and out on the hood. It was so cool and I got such a kick out of that. I was in heaven with all the rainbows. Then I heard Marc say, *"Look at the car, Ma."* The car was bright <u>orange</u>! I knew that Marc was with me, and he made my day with these signs and rainbows! Love ya, babe.

This is way more than I can believe…while looking through my papers I found an article that I had torn out of a magazine. It was about <u>quitting smoking</u>. Marc smoked and I wanted to send this article to him to read. I guess I never sent it because I knew in my heart that Marc probably wouldn't read it anyway. I had written the date on the top upper right in ink… 12/3/20. The note I wrote on the top left said, "Marc, I love you - Don't die before me. Love (heart) Mom. Marc died on 12/3/20!!!

MAY 9, 2021 - MOTHER'S DAY

All day long I felt Marc would send me a "gift" for Mother's Day. My niece called and came over for a visit. She walked in the door with a bouquet of yellow daisies and said, "Happy Mother's Day… I brought <u>flowers from Marc</u>." I was so happy and surprised. I knew he would send something for me today. We put them in with the roses that Adam and Brittany had sent me and they looked beautiful. Thank you, Marc, you are so sweet, and know that I love you. And thanks to Brittany and Adam for thinking of me today, too. How blessed am I?

Standing by the sink later that day, I started talking to Marc and told him thanks for the flowers which touched my heart. I know that he feels how much I want him to be safe and happy. He said to me, *"Don't worry, Mom, everybody here loves me."* Oh, OH, OH!!! Oh, Lord, I am so elated! This was his <u>best message</u> to me yet. No other words from him could give me the hope that this one sentence brought to me! Thank you, thank you, thank you! I felt such peace knowing that he is finally in a place of safety and unconditional love. Oh, that's so wonderful. My heart brightened with joy. What a Mother's Day blessing he gave me! I am so happy!

MAY 12, 2021

My friend, Donna, had called me and Andie a couple of days ago and wanted to have a video conference with us both. Her son had not been in contact with Donna for the last four years. It was such a painful part of life for her. Her son was gay and she was open to that, but he wanted nothing to do with Donna being his mother, even though she loved him with all her heart. Heartbroken, she moved to the beach to be by the sea. She walked the beach and had a daily ritual where she offered her son up to God. She didn't want to hold shame or hurt in her heart. It's been a rough four years for her not knowing if he is safe and well. Every mother needs to know that.

She and Andie do mediumship readings together and are very familiar with Marc's spirit. We have talked about him many times and Marc seems to want to hang out with Andie. When my gals did the reading for me, Marc came through loud and clear. Well, these two gals talked a few days ago to discuss how Donna can deal with Mother's Day. They prayed to God together, and then Andie asked Marc to help with changing this situation for the best and the highest good of all. Later, Marc told Andie, *"Wait till you see what I did!"*

Today, on Donna's son's birthday, I did our video call with Andie and Donna. Donna wanted to see our faces when she told us what had happened on Mother's Day. On that Sunday, Donna had gotten a phone call from her son! He wished her a Happy Mother's Day and said, "You know my friend <u>Marc with a "C"? He encouraged me to call my mother.</u> You remember him, he's Marc!?" Donna was floored and didn't remember any of her son's friends - but knew without a doubt who Marc with a "C" was! Andie and I were in shock and started to cry. Our friend was laughing and then we started laughing. No one could believe it! We were all so filled with joy and happiness for her. Andie told me the last time we talked that Marc was standing taller and prouder. He is so proud of what he did for Donna and so happy for both her and her son. Donna had said that she had prayed for "a card, and to know where he is, and to hear his voice". She got it all thanks to Marc with a "C"! Marc has become a "Spiritual Encourager". Thanks, Marc. Love you, honey. You are still bringing love and hope to everybody. If anybody could orchestrate a change of heart in another, we all knew you could. We love you and are so happy for you. Thanks from the bottom of our hearts.

MAY 22, 2021

While talking with Andie today, she said that Marc is something! He was singing "Smooth Operator" to her and she was laughing! I tuned in and heard him sing, <u>"Smooth Operation"</u>. How funny! I know this is about my surgery, and I thank you, Marc. I truly believe that Marc needed to leave so he could work with Spirit and help me from the other side. He is better able to help me from the afterlife than he could if he were still here. He is giving me strength. My upcoming back surgery is scheduled for May 26, in four days. I can't believe all the people I have praying for me, it's a massive number of prayers being sent my way. Donna sent me a prayer shawl that she knitted and her prayer group prayed over it for my recovery. Andie sent me a sherpa and velvet purple blanket with words of strength all over it. Lula sent me a sherpa and velvet white blanket with butterflies all over it, just like Marc's shirt he gave me for my birthday after he had passed! My surgery has brought so many people together in prayer. There's a wonderful light prayer group that has been holding me up to the highest energy. I feel so blessed and at peace with this. I am trusting that Jesus has me in the palm of his hands while Marc is at work behind the scenes. There is no need for me to worry. I'm covered in blessings. This surgery will be my transformation as I let go of any negative energy that I've been carrying on my back for so long. I heard Marc tell me, *"Your readings and Reiki healings are great, Ma, but they can't hold a candle to the light you will shine after you let go."* Wow, thanks!

MAY 24, 2021

Adam wanted to come out to stay here while I had my surgery, but I kept telling him that I'll be okay. Then I thought more about that, and I realized that I did want Adam here for my surgery. I called Adam at the last minute and he flew in from Arizona to be here with Denny for my surgery and hospitalization. That is such a blessing to me. I realize that he has to work while he's here, but he came as soon as I asked him to come. Thanks, Adam. You're the best!

Marc thanked Adam for coming here to help me and Denny… tonight when we went to the warehouse store, Adam walked in front of the TV speakers, they immediately came on the loudest they could and made so much noise until Adam walked away! It was so wild! Everybody was on high alert!! LOL. I knew right away it was Marc! He would definitely let Adam know he was with us by using giant speakers!

MAY 25, 2021

The phone has been ringing non-stop with people wishing me well and praying for me. My family and friends got this covered! I am so blessed. Tomorrow's my big day. My entire back will be broken… and my shell will be cracked open, too. I have been a turtle for far too long. I will finally release what needs to be let go. I am so grateful for all my support. Like Dad used to say, "If you can count your friends on the fingers of one hand, then you are blessed." Wow, I am blessed to the heavens!

MAY 26, 2021

Had my surgery today. Before I went under, I prayed with all my doctors and nurses and I sent Reiki healing energy to the operating room, staff, equipment, and everything else. I asked the angels to keep me safe. I feel Marc with me and I do not doubt that everything is as it should be and it's all good. I remember that the doctor came, asked me if I was ready, and wrote an "X" with a black magic marker on the back of my neck. After that... nothing. I was gone... and somewhere else. Ten hours later, with 3 rods and 42 pins down my entire spine, I was lying flat on my back in Intensive Care. I was in ICU for a short time and then they moved me to the floor, where my team of specialists watched my every breath and heartbeat. I remember that I could see and I could speak. That's about it.

I wonder where I was when everything went black. Was I with Marc and the angels?

JULY 30, 2021

Whoa! I don't have any memories of being in the hospital for 10 days, except that I was given a lot of blood, and apparently, a lot of drugs, thank God. I remember seeing Denny and Adam there once, although they were there with me every day. I remember three times when the nurses gave me more blood. I also remember that my eyes were looking around the room while my mind made the unfamiliar patterns I saw turn into faces! That was strange. I think that I was away in the world of Spirit with Marc. I wouldn't be surprised if I was on the other side for much of this time, although I remember none of it. Did I show up in Andie's kitchen? LOL, I'll have to ask her! So much has happened and I felt Marc with me the entire time.

After 11 days of rehab, I'm home recovering. The surgery went well. Adam returned home to Arizona while I was in rehab, and then Adam and Brittany both came out to help Denny and me for a couple of weeks while I was first at home, and we greatly appreciated their loving-kindness. My family and friends have been beyond angels. So much loving-kindness and blessings coming my way. Prayers, home-cooked meals, transportation, cards, letters, and calls from so many loved ones! I can't pick up a piece of paper, or take a deep breath, and my pain is unbelievable, but I know I'm blessed. I cannot BLT... bend, lift, or twist. I was given 12 pain pills and then told to take Tylenol. Seriously? (But, I get it!) I tell myself that when I am feeling my pain, I am feeling my healing and I do believe that. (And I never again want to hear anyone tell me that they have a hangnail!) Every day I try to do more. I have home-health nurses and therapists coming in to help me and teach me how to use all my adaptive equipment. I can do almost nothing but take a breath at this point, I can't even lift a pencil now, and I feel like a baby taking constant naps, but when I nap I feel Marc and the angels with me and I get so much comfort and hope. I can sit in a chair, or on the sofa. At night, I sleep in my new recliner. I can walk with a walker.

Denny and I sat on the porch this morning and it took me quite a time to walk out there. I'm using my walker and I'm super careful so that I will not fall. While we were sitting outside, we saw the guy who lives here who looks like Marc walking down the hill. That was Marc telling us that he is here with us! Thanks, Marc. Love you.

AUGUST 18, 2021

Yesterday at physical therapy they were playing 60's music and I was doing a hamstring stretch when "Bobby McGee" started to play. I remembered singing this and crying with Marc right before he crossed over. Then I felt Marc holding me tight and I lost it and started bawling, much to the concern of the PT staff!!. That was such a bittersweet moment, and I know Marc was telling me, *"You got this, Mom. It's all good."* I felt he was telling me that he was proud of me. Then I looked up at the wall and there was a rainbow and I didn't know where it came from! Thanks for sending me rainbows, Marc. They give me hope. Please, keep them coming!

SEPTEMBER 3, 2021

Today is Marc's birthday. Happy Birthday, Sweetie, we all miss you. This morning his sweet friend called and we talked. Her son was born on this day also, and she had lost him in December, just like Marc. We were truly soul sisters. We had a lovely conversation and wished both our sons a Happy Birthday as we cried! They are celebrating together now today!!

That night we had a birthday party for Marc and a few family and friends came. Lula had made the celebration special by bringing dinner and she hung a huge orange sign "Happy Birthday, Marc" on the wall and bought orange plates and tablecloths and it was so fun. Denny's nieces made it special, too. Everyone has been so loving. His cake said "Happy Birthday, Cark" and we sang and... and this was hysterical... we all waited for him to blow out his candles!!! That was so funny, but we would not have been surprised if it would have happened! Cark always surprises us! Everybody has been personally touched by all his signs and messages!

SEPTEMBER 11, 2021

Denny was feeling terrible and I called 911 for an ambulance as he needed to go to the emergency room., and it was super hard for me to get around, but I did it! After I made the call, I saw 3 big rainbows on our wall (and I have crystals in the window but it was a cloudy day), and I knew Marc was telling me that everything was going to be all right. (And everything was.). Thanks, Marc. Denny spent two days and nights in the hospital, and while he was away, his nieces slept on our sofa overnight with me. I have a wonderful family for which I am so grateful. I know how blessed I am.

SEPTEMBER 16, 2021

I watched the weather channel this morning and they showed a picture of a huge double rainbow that someone had sent them. I felt that was a good morning sign from Marc. It was beautiful. While I was praying my rosary this evening, I was listening to soft music on a TV station and a beautiful song came on and the title was "Afterglow". That's the verse that is on the back of all Marc's remembrance prayer cards! I felt him with me and everything was good. The signs keep coming, and I feel Marc here with me. Thanks, honey.

SEPTEMBER 22, 2021

Today is our wedding anniversary. The home phone rang this morning and Marc's name came up on the caller ID. When I answered, there was nobody on the line! I knew it was Marc wishing Denny and me a happy anniversary. Thanks, Marc. You're so sweet.

After my evening shower, Denny (my helper and angel) tossed my used washcloth into the sink and all kinds of rainbow bubbles floated up into the air! At first, I thought that it was Marc telling us happy anniversary again, but then I realized that it was Marc telling us that he is with Pap, because Pap's favorite song to sing was "I'm Forever Blowing Bubbles"! Thanks, Marc. That's so comforting knowing that you're with Pap and Gram.

SEPTEMBER 26, 2021

A beautiful rainbow appeared in our "office" right under the framed explanation of the name "Joy". It was so lovely. It was on the wall right next to the window, so I knew that it didn't come from the window. I knew Marc had sent it and I thanked him.

I saw the brightest rainbow on the wall tonight in our bedroom and there was no sunshine. It was next to my rainbow night light. I know it was Marc telling me that it's all good. Thanks, honey.

SEPTEMBER 30, 2021

I was in a room getting an electrocardiogram because I have been having chest pains. I just feel that it's stress - my mind and body have been through the wringer. I saw Marc come to the foot of the exam table with Denny's dog MeMe and she jumped up on the bed and wagged her tail and was excited to see me! They were telling me that everything is good (and it was). Marc told me that MeMe is driving him crazy, always around him, and won't let him be! That's MeMe. Marc just laughed and shook his head because she is so needy! But I know he loves her and is taking good care of her while she is with him.

Tonight <u>Denny's phone called my phone</u> while he was sleeping in bed and I was sleeping in my new recliner! Hi, Marc! We love you. But please don't wake us up like that anymore!

OCTOBER 10, 2021

Today was a beautiful day of 79 degrees with a slight breeze. Denny took me to the cemetery to visit Marc's "penthouse", and to walk (slowly) down the lane to see Gram and Pap's "pencil case'. (Dad called their burial niche the "pencil case" because it was a deep niche with room for two caskets. He used to tell Mom "whoever dies first will go to the back of the "pencil case". Dad's in the back.) We parked by the maintenance garage and there was a humongous ten-foot butterfly bush all covered with purple blooms. It was gorgeous. I took a couple of pictures of it because it had bright orange butterflies all over the blooms. The butterflies reminded me of Marc. The bush looked like it was alive! Those butterflies had Marc's good energy. It was an awesome experience. Well, I could hardly believe it, but <u>his energy showed up in all the photos</u>. He was one giant swoop across the picture of the bush. It was so sweet of him to thank us for remembering him here at his "penthouse". It was so peaceful there today. I heard a boat/train <u>whistle</u> down over the hill and that's my psychic sign for peace - that everything is better than ever before and it's all good. Marc was so reassuring today.

OCTOBER 25, 2021

Last night I had <u>a dream</u>. I was very high on a hill and I looked down at the valley below that was miles deep and I got scared to death. On this hill, I saw a hand-dug grave with a headstone and rocks around it. Next to it was a smaller grave with rocks around it. Then I was over the hill clinging to the side but it was like sand and I couldn't get a grip. I kept clawing my way to the top and finally, I made it out and over.

Denny's daughter called me this morning. She was crying because Marc's dog Abby had crossed over. She's going to bury her wrapped in Marc's orange blanket out in the backyard. I feel so sad for Den's daughter, she was the best pet mom Abby could ever have. But, I'm happy for Marc, because all his "pet crew" is with him now and everything feels complete. Then I thought about my dream last night. Marc was giving me a "heads up". Those graves were Marc's and Abby's. We couldn't have funerals so both graves were hand-dug. Marc's "penthouse" is high on a hill. Sometimes I feel like I'm "over the hill", trying to claw my way back to the top while I heal (hill) from this back surgery. Marc, I'm so glad that Abby is with you now. I feel like you are complete now and it's all good. We can all relax.

NOVEMBER 20, 2021

Denny's daughter called. She was a victim of road rage at a fast-food drive-thru. Some guy hit her car 4 times. He just kept banging into her. Then she started to cry. She cried because of this crazy guy hitting her, and cried over not having Marc. Then she cried because Abby was gone, and as long as she had Abby, she felt she also had Marc. She was sobbing and we both were crying together. I felt like it would be so nice for her to have Abby to hold. Then <u>Marc told me</u> to *"Give her the heart"*. What heart? Then it hit me. When we were at my last surgeon's appointment, we went to the hospital gift shop and I bought a weighted heart that could be warmed and held. I had seen it on a TV shopping channel for twice the cost. I bought it because it was such a good price, although I did not know if I wanted it or to whom I might want to give it to. That happens a lot with me, I buy something without knowing why, and then something happens and lets me know that I bought it to help a person through some hard time. The Universe always gives me the person who needs it! Anyway, Marc told me to give that to Den's daughter because it was the size and weight of Abby and she could warm it up and cuddle with it. She needed to feel like she was holding Abby again. How beautiful was that? Thanks, Marc for the heads up. Love you.

NOVEMBER 25, 2021

Happy Thanksgiving. It's been a year since we last saw Marc at Thanksgiving and I was missing him. I got my morning coffee, went to the TV, and put on the Thanksgiving Day parade. There was a big marching band in rows, all dressed as caterpillars. Then they all went under this huge white tarp and when they came out they were all big orange butterflies spreading their wings! It took my breath away, it meant so much to me! That was Marc, telling me he is here with me just like at the butterfly bush. That was so beautiful, I got chills and started crying. His death was not the end of the world. It was <u>his unveiling and metamorphosis</u> into an amazing new beginning. He's not dead, he's like the caterpillar… he's just changed form and is more beautiful now than ever. Thanks, Marc. You are not gone - you just have evolved into something more amazing. You are my precious orange butterfly and I love you more than you'll ever know… or I'm sure you do know!

NOVEMBER 28, 2021

At night when I pray the rosary, I listen to the TV music channel. Tonight there was a picture of a starry night and the song playing was called "Reunion". Marc told me again that he was a star in the sky and I should look up and <u>see him when I see the stars</u>. So every night I go outside on the porch and see him in a star and I feel him with me. We talk and I keep telling him what I need. I know he's working behind the scenes for me. What a comfort, knowing he's the stuff of stars and we can always be together. Thanks, Marc. Love you.

So tonight I went out to look at the stars and it seemed that there were none, but I could see some out of the corner of my eye. I started to cry and told Marc, "I can see you and I know that you're with me." I asked him to hold me and hug me and I felt his arms around me. I came into the house and the TV music channel was on and the song playing was "Chrysalis"!!! That's what I saw in the Thanksgiving Day parade when all the caterpillars transitioned into orange butterflies when they came out from under the tarp. It wasn't the end of their lives. It was a new beginning. That's Marc - now an orange butterfly! So beautiful. The very next song that played was "Bright Silence in C sharp"... Marc with a "C"!!!

We've changed the clocks to "fall back". Hate it. Anyhow, the clock Marc bought us when we retired that has all the numbers tumbled on the bottom and says "Whatever" is not working anymore! Marc told me, *"There's no time here. Just be happy and enjoy whatever time you think you have. Time is an illusion. It is so wonderful not to be governed by linear thoughts of time. Enjoy your life. Be happy. I am happy. That's what I want for you."* Thanks, Marc. Xoxo. Then I asked Marc where he lives on the other side and he told me, *"Wherever there is snow."* He always loved the snow and wanted to move to Denver. How sweet it is to hear his voice.

NOVEMBER 29, 2021

Sometimes my mind goes to places where I don't belong. It's not like I'm the only one on this planet who has that problem. Thank God I have great friends whom I can share intimate conversations with. They tell me like it is and I am so receptive to that. Everyone needs to be put back on the right track every now and then. I know that I have so much to learn.

Andie called and said she talked to Marc in the morning and he told her that he loves to talk to these "Old Fart Mediums" (me, Andie, and my friends)! She laughed because she knew that those weren't her words! Marc said that he is sending guidance to us all. He said to pay attention to the signs he sends, and any ideas we might get, no matter how crazy! We need to become aware of how we feel because if we feel him with us, he is with us because our feelings are accurate. These are all the important ways that Spirit and those who have crossed over will communicate with us. He wants everybody to start noticing what they call coincidences in their lives. There are no coincidences. These are signs from Spirit and that's called synchronicity because there is no apparent cause for these things to happen. He wants everybody to know this. Marc said, *"Pay attention! Your loved ones are sending you messages of hope and love. They are in a good place of peace and bliss. They are always with you and can be in many places at once. And, don't worry, they don't watch you take a shower, they just connect with your energy. It's all good."*

NOVEMBER 30, 2021

I was watching a television shopping network and they were selling kitchen equipment and cookware. The guy on the show was making a <u>frittata</u>. I started laughing. It reminded me of a happy and fun story that Marc's neighbor had told me. Marc was very close to her because she had a stroke, and Marc looked out for her and helped her. Those two were best buds. She said that when she first introduced Marc to her pre-school-aged granddaughter, Marc asked her granddaughter what she had done that day. She told him that she went to school. He told his neighbor that he thought she was adorable. He kept on talking to her. Then he asked her what she did in school that day. She said that they made a frittata today. He about fell over that a pre-schooler knew how to make a frittata, let alone say it! He and his neighbor laughed about that for years! It was a great story, and hearing the TV guy cooking a frittata isn't a coincidence. It's a synchronicity. All things happen for a reason. I know you are here with me now, Marc. Thanks for making me laugh!

Marc's SWOOP is with us at the butterfly bush!

CHAPTER 22

TIME IS AN ILLUSION

DECEMBER 3, 2021

Today is the first anniversary of Marc's crossing over. I can't believe it's been a year, but Marc reassures me that there is no "time" on the other side. I thought about his crossing over last night, and I cried for myself because I'm missing him, and then I realized that if I had died before him, I wouldn't want him to be sad and I would want to comfort him. He is totally free and I am sure of that. Knowing that is such a blessing. I just hate that he's not here to hug. Sometimes it hurts so bad and I feel empty.

I wasn't sure how I would handle this day. Lula took me shopping today just to get me out of the house. I'm so glad my best friend cares so much about me. I think that I would have had a hard time if I would have stayed at home all day. We went "gyppin" around together and I was so happy. We went to the store to buy Christmas presents and jerseys for Denny with logos from his favorite sports teams. The young guy who waited on us was named "Frank". What are the chances he would have Pap's name? Who names their son "Frank" anymore? But it was so cool, again <u>Marc's telling me he's with Pap</u>.

On our drive home, the most get-outta-here experience happened. The sun was setting and the sky turned a beautiful golden yellow and watery-blue and it was super-odd. Like "end of the world" odd. The sunset resembled the beach and the ocean in the distance. Strangely beautiful! Then we were amazed to see the trees and the road and the houses all turn to brighter-than-the-sun orange! <u>NEON ORANGE WAS EVERYWHERE</u>, and Lula almost drove the car off the road! We couldn't believe it. It was orange, magnified a million times! I took a couple of pictures and everybody was shocked. That bright neon orange world lasted about 15 minutes. I don't know if it was just meant for us to see or if anyone else saw it. At least Lula saw it and I know I'm not crazy. It was unbelievable! Gas stations, churches, road signs, everything was orange! Wow, Marc! Blowing my mind! Thanks, Marc, what greater validation can I get than you turning the world into electric orange for the anniversary of your birthing-into-spirit day. This is one sign I can never forget. I thought that I was in the orange twilight zone! So cool! How wonderful for you to show us how happy you are in the afterlife. I know you're good! That orangey world you made for us is so unbelievable! Thanks!

DECEMBER 6, 2021

This is so strange. I had sent Andie a Christmas gift package of pure goat milk bath products because she has been such a sweetheart and has helped me in so many ways. She also shares the messages that Marc gives to her for me and that's so reassuring. Her gift contained my favorite goat mild products that I love and I bought it from a TV shopping network that has been my godsend this Christmas time. I figured that since I loved it, Andie would like it too, because we both like the same things most of the time. (I'm not about to go "gyppin" around in the cold and snow to buy presents, and my stamina is still set to low. I don't think I even can at this point. Walking takes a ton of energy from me at this point.) Anyway, Andie's gift was supposed to be delivered to her a week ago. Every single day, I called her and asked her if she has received her package and she told me she had not. Finally today I asked her again. She said no. So I called the shopping network and a guy named "Frank" (AGAIN! Are you kidding me?) told me that it had been delivered and the date it was delivered. I told him that she didn't receive it and he told me they will send her a replacement free of charge. That was terrific and I was glad. I called Andie back and told her that I had called the TV network and she's getting another goat milk gift set.

She said, "Oh… oh, are you talking about the goat milk gift package from the shopping network? Yes, I did get it. I was confused because you had just sent me a package with some of Marc's jewelry and I knew that I had received that. But this goat milk package came on the day after my kids sent me a goat milk shampoo and conditioner gift set, so I got confused. There was no card, so I asked the kids if they had sent it to me and they told me no. I didn't know who sent it." (WHAT???? HELLO!!!! Meanwhile, I'm asking her every day about receiving a package!)

We both started laughing because we both thought we were losing it. So I told her that she was getting a replacement gift. Then I heard Marc say, *"Tell her that it's a birthday present from me."* I thought that Marc must have meant "Christmas present", but, as always I relayed what he told me (I never question Spirit because they are always right!) I asked her when her birthday was because I had no idea. Her birthday is in a couple of weeks! Marc was spot on! Marc sent us both a ton of laughter today. We can't believe <u>Marc is sending presents</u> to us<u>!</u> It's great!

There are a lot of "Franks" in my world lately. Today on TV, there was a commercial with a man named "Frank". "Frank" was written on the front of his tee-shirt. I knew that it was Dad telling me that Marc is with him. I wondered if they were really together on the other side. Then <u>Dad said to me</u>, "Do you believe that Marc is here with me?" I answered, "Yes". "Do you trust me to take good care of him?" I answered, "Absolutely". "Then let go of the worry and know that we are together. I got this. I came before him so that I could be here for him." It was so good to hear Dad's voice again. Thank you, thank you, thank you, Dad and God, for giving me hope and peace.

DECEMBER 7, 2021

Remember the goat milk package mix-up with Andie when she ended up with two of the gift sets? Well, she called me today and put her daughter, who is also a psychic medium, on the phone and we all talked together. Her daughter was all excited. She had received a gift of goat milk products packaged in an advent box, and it's one where you opened one little window with a surprise product every day until Christmas. She was so thrilled because she's a goat milk gal, too. She called her husband to thank him, and he had no idea what she was talking about. Then she called Andie to thank her, but she hadn't sent her daughter a gift. She and Andie were so confused. They called me to tell me the story. Nobody, including me, knew where that package came from - there was no card. I thought this was funny. Then it got crazy when her daughter asked me if Marc was tall. (He was 6'3"). She said that she was in her bathroom when she heard her front door open and close and when in her mind's eye, she saw a very tall man walk in and sit on her sofa and cross his ankle over his thigh. (That's so Marc.). He had his arm over the top of the sofa and was so relaxed. She said he is so content and happy, and that he could never be that way when he was in his body on Earth. He wanted her to know the great peacefulness that he feels! He's always with her. We all agreed that <u>Marc had sent Andie's daughter the gift package</u>! We don't know how, but this is no coincidence. She knows that it will be a charge on her credit card, but she is left in suspense as to how it got into her online shopping cart! Thanks, Marc. I'm so glad that you're happy. It's so funny that he's connected to Andie's family and that he's doing all this gift shopping for them! Leave it to Cark! He loves to give presents!!

    Then that night, I was in the bathroom washing my hands (We mediums must do all our connecting while we are in the bathroom!?!), and I thought of the sensual scent of my favorite goat milk moisturizer and then I realized that I had ordered body creams and I never received them. I looked for them but couldn't find them where I had them in the drawer. I called the shopping network again and told them I never received the package. They told me it had been delivered, but they will send me a replacement. I was thinking that Marc orchestrated all this goat milk gift stuff with Andie and her daughter to remind me about that delivery that I didn't receive. Thanks for the heads-up, Marc. Love you.

DECEMBER 15, 2021

You will never believe this!!!! Today my goat milk body creams replacement package was delivered. All because I never received the first one. I took them out of the box and went into the bedroom to put them into the drawer and I saw a box of body creams already in there!!! Dear Lord!! I DID receive the first package, but I was positive that I hadn't. It wasn't in the drawer when I looked for it the other day! Marc had made it invisible! That had to be <u>Marc sending me a birthday and Christmas present</u>! Oh, Lordy! Thanks so much, Marc. I was sure that I didn't receive them! He's sending us all presents. He loves to gift others! I can't believe that all this wonderful goat milk stuff is coming from Cark.

Marc told me to quit trying so hard in this life. He told me to just be, and allow others to be. That everything is playing out as it should. That I don't need to help anybody unless they come to me and ask me directly. He said that where I am now is exactly where I'm supposed to be and so is everybody else. Don't waste your energy and go with the flow. It's all good. Then he told me to find joy in little things and to do what brings me joy. He told me to wash my hands with the sensual goat milk body wash because I love that scent so much! Marc told me to use it in every soap dispenser because I so enjoy the aroma. He wants me to enjoy simple pleasures, which I need to do more often.

DECEMBER 16, 2021

I have been bothered by the fact that the network shopping channel sent two gifts that should not have been sent because we had already received them. There's money that needs to be paid for these items, but I feel like an idiot calling the network again. They'll call me crazy and won't answer the phone anymore when they see my name!! But I have a feeling that the money for these gifts needs to go somewhere. Money is energy, and it needs to be balanced. Someone else should benefit besides all us gals. I sat in my recliner and thought about how to set this straight. I wondered who I should give the money to for Andie's and my gift sets and I heard Marc tell me, *"Humane Society"*. Okay, yes, he had given donations to them when I was with him. He loves his animals. So I sent a large check to the Humane Society to balance the energy of the two goat milk gifts we had received as replacements. I wrote them a note and sent the money in memory of Marc. When I licked the envelope, I heard Marc say, *"Thanks for my Christmas present, Mom."* Oh, how wonderful! Marc had sent five presents; Andie got a present, her daughter got a gift, I got a present, Marc got a present, and the animals got a present, too! Presents all around! Oh, how sweet! This was all Marc's doing! Merry Christmas to all!

DECEMBER 21, 2021

Andie, Elizabeth, and I got together for a video card reading with some of our other friends. Nobody else showed up. We don't get excited because everything works out as it should. So just the three of us pulled cards for each other. Elizabeth feels like Marc is our group spirit guide. We always feel his energy and he always seems to show up in our readings. I agree. He loves his "old fart mediums"! I pulled a card for Elizabeth from a new deck I had just bought. The top of the card said, "Be Playful". There was a generic picture in the middle of the card. The bottom of that card said, "Be Playful and Masturbate." We about fell over laughing. I told Elizabeth that's exactly what she needs! It was too funny. We laughed for twenty minutes! She asked me to pull another card. I kid you not... the next card I pulled showed a picture of a sculptor and the top of the card said, "Use Your Hands". We laughed until we cried! We think Marc had something to do with this!! Too funny! Good time with friends and Spirit!!!

DECEMBER 24, 2021

My birthday. My Sweetie, Denny, brought me the apple pie that I asked for instead of a birthday cake. He had gone to pick up the pie at the store earlier in the morning and asked the gal to put a little sign that said "Happy Birthday" on the top of the pie. He's so sweet. When he came home, he told me to sit down because he had a story to tell me. After he bought the pie at the grocery store, he was walking out of the doors when he heard someone say to him, *"WHOA - You're forgetting something."* He turned around to see who was talking to him but nobody was around him. He heard it again. He was wondering what was going on. Then he remembered that he wanted to buy me a cupcake, too. So, he went back and bought it. He said that it was from Marc. How sweet was it for my honey and Marc to make my birthday special? I am thrilled. Denny still can't believe it. I think that he was spooked. I agree that it is unnerving to hear words from the other side. Thanks for reminding him, Marc, and for my lovely little cake.

DECEMBER 28, 2021

Christmas is over and it was nice. Spent with family and friends. Marc sent us rainbows on the walls all day, and it wasn't even sunny! Although Adam and Britt's flight was canceled, they have already made plans to come out for Easter. We are good with that and know that there was a reason they couldn't get here now. It's disappointing but we accept the way it is because we can't do anything about it. We'll just open Christmas gifts in April.

DECEMBER 29, 2021

I was confused because I felt angry today. It still comes and goes and I know I have been carrying it since I first read Marc's official cause of death. Although it was ruled accidental, it was such a shock to me. I felt like Marc died twice. My feelings have been crazy ever since I read that death certificate. I still have questions and wish I had answers but know I will get none. There were so many reasons that I felt angry. I am mostly angry that Marc keeps telling me that everything is okay. He tells me that all the time. Yeah, there in heaven it's grand… but I'm here on Earth and the story of your death hurts me so. You were murdered. I am so mad. You were no angel. My heart is so broken that I never wanted to see the truth of you being on drugs. I could have never helped you. I felt like I was walking on glass. I avoided your pain pill addiction like the plague. I just couldn't deal with it, it was just painful to see you mess up your life. But, what do I know? No matter how I feel now it's just because I love you so much. I need to understand so many things. I want to see more of the big picture now...

I am judging my actions.
I am judging your actions.
I could not, in any way, help you.
You were trying to lessen the pain.
I was trying to lessen the pain.
I need to quit judging anything.
I don't know your story.
I don't know my story, how could I know anybody else's?
It was your time to go.
So many people love you.
You are so very good to others.
You were no angel.
Nobody is an angel, including me.
Other people who love you are angry and sad.
It's over and I forgive myself for being unable to help you.
It's over and I forgive you for the way you lived and died.
It's over and I forgive myself for wanting you to live your life differently.
If I hurt you, I am sorry.
What do I know?
You were on your own journey.
I'm happy that you're free now.
I gotta do a lot of work to get over this pain.
I need to be happy because you're in a great place now.
I'm happy you have evolved.
Only the present moment counts.
You're here. I'm here. We're both together and safe.
You are a wonderful being of love.
It's all good, no matter how I feel.

I realize that grief sucks, big time. I am stuck in the middle of this process of letting go. My son was murdered and his life is over. There are so many different emotions entangled in the process of grieving. I am allowed to feel sad and get angry. It's very sane of me to feel anger, shame, and pain. It's all a part of grieving. I am on a journey of looking inward. I'm diving deep into the ocean of my emotions. Of facing my feelings head-on. Of loving both my joy and my anger. I am healing. I need to be gentle with myself.

DECEMBER 31, 2021

Happy New Year. I need a Happy New Year more than anybody could know. But the good news is that time heals. And I made it this far with no drugs to mess up my mind and give me false hope. I give myself credit for feeling my feelings without taking a pill. I felt the emotional pain when I needed to, and I'm moving on. Better days are ahead. Life sometimes punches me in the face now, but I know it will not be for long. Grief is a process. This too shall pass. I'm kinda glad that I am dealing with the physical healing of my back during this period of grieving. Sometimes the pain gives me something else to focus on besides Marc's passing.

Joy Elaine Reed

CHAPTER 23

LIGHT WORKERS

JANUARY 2, 2022

Zara called and gave me much to think about. I love how wise she is. She said that I am in a void now. It'll be a rough journey for me but it will be all good. I feel as if this is my time for physical and spiritual healing. I do feel more unattached to everything. I feel as if once you lose a child, why be attached to anything? Nothing matters like it did before. I am more aware now and I can give up all control and just be the observer. I see through others' behaviors and know when what they say and what they do are two different things. In my body, my back muscles are really tight but the swelling has gone down a ton. Physically, my pain is extreme. I feel very different now... physically, mentally, emotionally, and spiritually. I am healing, but healing hurts on all levels.

JANUARY 4, 2022

Denny and I went to Lula's for dinner. She has been an amazing friend and has provided home cooking since my surgery. We are so blessed. I love her dearly for who she is. She is so caring and always shines her light to others. After we ate, we had coffee and watched the dog show on TV. We saw a large, black standard poodle with a poodle cut that looked like Denny's little poodle who had passed on, and I said, "Look, Denny, it's a big MeMe." As he looked, the dog's name flashed on the screen... something, something, something, Afterglow!! That's the verse on the back of

Marc's prayer cards! MeMe is with Marc! It was so nice to get this sign from them both!

JANUARY 22, 2022

It's been a little over a year since Marc has passed. I began to write his book after the new year started and I have finished writing the first chapter of the book. This is a good time to start the book because I feel Marc is with me. So are Mom and Dad. He's not sending me a lot of signs anymore like he used to. He's being more philosophical now. But his sweet energy is always around me and I recognize it immediately. And, I keep getting "Frank" on TV. He's with dad and they're gyppin' around together in that Great Beyond.

I feel that Marc is busy with a global project that will benefit the world. Although he is sending fewer signs, I don't seem to need his signs to feel encouraged anymore. I've realized that Marc is in the realm of total unconditional peace, love, and bliss. What more could I want? I go into my mind, and I'm with him. He bends forward and hugs me tight. He is my "Joy Guide" who brings the departed souls that want to communicate with my clients. He is still best friends with Andie and her daughter. It's all good. (Just now, the Peter Max heart painting in the dining room began to rattle. I heard Marc say, "*I will never leave you, Mom. I love you.*" I love you, too, Marc.)

Tonight I had my first dream about Marc. I had waited over a year for this!!! I dreamed Marc and I were dancing together and I rubbed my hand over his shaved head and I felt the stubble and I smelled his scent. It was so wonderful and was something I had been praying for. Thanks for meeting me in my dreams, Marc. Xoxoxo. I feel so blessed and at peace.

JANUARY 27, 2022

Marc is still sending rainbows to me… on the table, on the walls, in the laundry room! The rainbows haven't stopped and I so appreciate seeing them.

FEBRUARY 4, 2022

Andie called. She said her daughter (whom I love so much and I have adopted!!) told her about a powerful presence in her house. He is tall and plays with the animals. He stood at her bed and grinned at her. She knew that she knew him and felt like it was Marc. Then her daughter's son had a dream about a tall guy in a townhouse who had all kinds of collections. (Marc). There was a box and both he and his mom did not want to look through it. Andie said it's filled with the stuff that I don't want to pull out and look at. Her grandson said that the man's presence was very strong. Marc's coming to them because he knows how close Andie and I are. Andie says, "We just got Carked!" when he comes to us. I guess I still have things to pull out of the box and deal with.

FEBRUARY 10, 2022

I am writing every day now and it feels effortless to me, and I know that Spirit and Marc are writing the book and using me as a channel. Words just appear on the pages and I am so grateful that they are "taking over" and using me. Some words make me laugh, and some make me cry, and I know that I need them all. Writing is a great release. Even writing about nothing, in particular, would be helpful to me and anybody else in grief and pain.

FEBRUARY 13, 2022

I talked to Marc today. We discussed how he died. I felt as if I had accepted him having an "aneurysm" better than an "overdose", even though his death was accidental.

He told me, *"So many people have addictions. Alcohol, sex, shopping, food, drugs, hoarding, gambling, people-pleasing, and other addictions and compulsions are the ways that make people feel safe in their world. It's their only form of pleasure. Addictions influence your brain. Addiction becomes a chronic disease that hijacks your brain. Stigma and shame are associated with addictions, especially using drugs.*

"More people die from addictions to prescribed medications than traffic accidents and gun deaths combined. It shatters your sense of security. And, now that the drug dealers are making pills with fentanyl that look like prescribed medications, the leading cause of death in 20-year-olds through 45-year-olds is fentanyl poisoning."

"Addictions stem from trauma and we all react to trauma in different ways. Post Traumatic Stress Disorder causes people to remain in psychological shock and then they are unable to process their emotions. Although we all need help, addicts especially need to choose to do activities that may be beneficial; exercise and walk, don't isolate themselves, and be with the people who make them feel comfortable. Ask for support from people who don't judge you. Stay social. Reconnect with old friends. Feel your feelings. Take care of your body; do not engage in your addictions, sleep when you need it, eat clean, and do yoga and relaxation techniques. Focus on the body and not on thoughts or memories. Get the emotions and anger out. Hit the bed with a clothes hanger and scream until it's out of you. Drive your car to some isolated location and blast the radio and sing to your heart's content. Go to a 12-step meeting and listen, for perhaps the first time in your life. Ask for help. Do something to release the hurt. Do whatever it takes. It's your journey and if you want to be happy... go for it. KNOW THAT IT'S NOT YOUR FAULT. Your brain has been re-wired by your addiction and it's difficult to fix it on your own."

FEBRUARY 15, 2022

Marc came to me. He told me, "You have nothing to do with my being gay. For years you have blamed yourself. Don't blame yourself, there is no blame here. I chose to be born gay. This was my journey, not yours. I picked you to be my mother because I knew that you would always love me, no matter what. I will always love you. Just like your mother wasn't responsible for the choices that you made in your life, you're not responsible for mine. There is no blame so stop beating yourself up. You're the best mom ever. Please tell all the moms and dads not to blame themselves. Let it all go. Everyone's on their own journey."

"No shame, please. Shame is based on the judgments of others and does not matter. Nothing is good or bad... it just is. So how can anyone judge? Be above the opinions of others because it's just an illusion. Change your tears of sadness, shame, and blame into tears of joy. I was born to shine the light of love on the oneness of the world. I did that, and then I left. Now I am home. My earthly life may be over, but I still have the same work to do here."

Marc made me realize that all that pain I went through in his life did not make me a better mother. I was a good mother, to begin with. That was his journey, not mine.

Marc told me, *"You're like an expensive bra, Ma. Your job is to lift and support! That's what a Light Worker does, and you're a super Light Worker. When you leave here and come home, you will be together with all the Light Workers like yourself... that's heaven, Ma. Heaven or hell is being together for all eternity with people just like you! That's a scary thought, isn't it? I hope it makes some people stop and think about their actions. You will one day be with me in Heaven. Make yourself happy while you're on Earth because nobody else can. Don't live somebody else's life because when you cross over... their life will flash before your eyes, and you don't want THAT to happen! LOL. Live your dreams. Enjoy yourself. Allow others to live their own drama. Everyone's on their own journey."*

I thanked Marc for all the wisdom he gave me. I needed to hear these words. He told me how it is, and I believe him because I know that, from where he is, he sees the big picture. I don't need to judge myself. I played my part in his life to the best of my ability. I was whom he needed me to be in his life. I was happy that he picked me. It all played out as it should. Marc knows everything now that he's on the other side. I appreciated his help and advice. He's become quite the philosopher and bra expert.

FEBRUARY 23, 2022

It was very early in the morning while I was waiting for the sun to switch on its earthly light when I had serious misgivings about writing this book. The book and its words were constantly churning throughout my mind and I wondered if this book was even remotely legit. It was difficult to imagine myself as an author. How will I find a publisher? I need a book cover! What should I do next? Who will read this book?... blah, blah, blah. My monkey brain was going wild! I was quickly descending into the crevasse of self-doubt. Marc must have seen where my thoughts were headed and he immediately came to my rescue. We had an important conversation and he gave me good advice...

"Good morning, Ma. I love you. It's time to "wake up" and drop the negativity. It's okay for you to feel confused and question your efforts. (Laughs) You're coming out as an author just as I came out as my true self so many years ago. Now you know how I felt for many years! I want you to know that you're in a good place and have no need to fear. The book has great energy and the power to heal. It's all good. The publishing of this book will take care of itself when the time is right. Flush that negativity down the toilet, woman! You have no control over who will read the book, but I can guarantee that it will get into the hands of the people who are ready to heal. Spirit has that covered one hundred percent. Chillax!"

I knew that Marc was right. "Thanks, Marc, I needed to hear that. Sometimes I get wrapped up in fear and I need to remember that it's not about me and to "let go my ego". I know that I must trust Spirit to lead me forward and to go with the flow downstream. There are so many dangling loose ends and my problem is that I want them all brought together now and tied into a neat bow. I am very impatient now. Adam always asks me, "How do you eat an entire elephant?" Yeah, yeah, one bite at a time… but I keep forgetting that. I need to do first things first, be patient, and deal with each loose end one at a time. There is a time for everything and I know when the time is right that all my concerns will be divinely addressed. Then the healing of others will begin. Thanks for waking me up, honey!"

"No problem. You're right on track and doing what you need to do. You know the bottom line is that no matter what plane we exist on, we are both Light Workers and are here to help others. TO CHANGE BUT ONE LIFE ON EARTH FOR THE BETTER IS THE ULTIMATE GOAL OF EVERY LIGHT WORKER. The greatest gift of Spirit is to allow you to raise the vibration of others. It is accomplished when you provide the RAINBOW POWER of support, kindness, understanding, selflessness, caring, compassion, and love. Those attributes are vibrations of love and they are all different colors! They are the colors of the rainbows I send you! Support is red. Kindness is orange. Understanding is yellow. Selflessness is green. Caring is blue. Compassion is indigo, and love is violet. When you envelop one person in all the colors of this healing rainbow, you are creating hope. That's the true power of the rainbow! You are a rainbow, Mom! You've written this book to bring rainbow light to others. The precious fulfillment of hope for just one person on earth is beyond your worldly comprehension, Mom. It's magnificent and astounding... and I wish you could see it from where I am. When a person is brought out of the dark and realizes the unconditional love of Spirit in their life for the first time - it's like birthing a newborn baby. It's party time and the number one cause for celebration on this side. LIVING A LIFE THAT CAN CREATE A POSITIVE CHANGE IN ANOTHER'S LIFE AND GIVE THEM HOPE IS THE GOAL. We're doing just that, Mom. You are sharing our story and I am so grateful to you! You have no idea how light this makes my energy! I know you can see me glowing in rainbow hues. It's so cool!"

He certainly was styling in rainbow hues and he was beautiful. "Honey, I never realized the colors of the rainbow were so powerful! I knew that the rainbow was a sign of hope, but I never thought about the power each hue held. That's amazing. It's no wonder you waved a rainbow flag! You're teaching me so much! Thanks, sweetie. I so appreciate your kindness. I know it's my grateful heart that fuels the rainbow power within me, and gratitude is the key. If I wasn't thankful for my continuing blessings, I would have zero hope. So much has been removed from my life, but so much remains and many more blessings have been added. For this I am thankful. I just want others to find this hope."

"Mom, you can't even imagine our book's influence on others. While on earth, it's difficult to see the magnitude of your effort. Mom, I'm telling you that my messages that you shared will create a ripple effect of major proportions throughout the Universe. Love is given, that love is accepted, and that same love is passed on and on and on and on to every person without end."

I was so glad that Marc came to me and lifted my energy. I went from feeling hopeless to being optimistic in five minutes, and I'm grateful that he's still encouraging people from the other side. Marc's message gave me hope that our book will be read by all those who are grieving or in pain. His words today filtered through me from the top of my head to my toes, and I could see myself standing under a waterfall with a rainbow wrapping around me. I never knew that a rainbow carried so much meaning! He was encouraging me to move forward and finish our tome. I wished that I could be wherever he was to see the ripple effect of our love in action. It seemed so awesome when I thought about all these unending ripples sending our love out farther and farther into the Universe. In my heart, I felt those ripples shine with every color of the rainbow! I became excited and hopeful. Our sweet conversation was my sign from Marc to keep on keeping on!

FEBRUARY 26, 2022

I was searching the internet for the phrase Marc with a "C"……and I found a photo of his coffee cup that said "Cark" that Marc posted on his social media page. It was all over the internet, people loved it years ago and they love it now. In fact, a tabloid newspaper in the UK did an article that was entitled "I said my name was Marc with a C" and it shared Marc's social media picture that he posted! I'm so shocked! Marc with a "C" is a celebrity!!!! How special! Good for you, honey! That's so cool! I always knew you had a big following!! You shall forever be known by your coffee cup!

MARCH 1, 2022

I had a long talk with Andie today, and we talked about Marc's book and the book about her family that she is writing. We are book buddies, both writing our memoirs. She told me that some of her family will see things differently than the stories she relates in her memoir, and she was concerned. I told her that everyone sees things through the filter of their lives and that no two people will have the same understanding of the details in her book. The experience is singular, and it's all flowing through the reader's eyes and life experiences. How people feel has no effect on our stories. We are just sharing what's true for us. I told her that, in my case, I worried that Adam would feel hurt because here I am, writing a story about his brother, and there Adam is, being so loving, but not getting a book written about him. I wondered how Adam would feel about that. I know in my heart that Adam knows that I love him more than all the stars in the Universe. Adam really has no reason to doubt my love for him just because I wrote this book. Adam is so very precious to me. I love him with all my heart and soul and being. Period. There we were again, in the dark alleys of our minds, worrying about everybody's reactions. Andie and I laughed about all the crazies we get when we think about publishing our stories. We can't wait to be on the New York Times best-seller list! OH, YES WE WILL!

Joy Elaine Reed

CHAPTER 24

BUBBLES OF LOVE

MARCH 8, 2022

Marc came to me this morning. He knew I had something on my mind. He wanted to clear up some issues. I told him that I loved him and asked him what he wanted to discuss.

"Addictions. They are tricky and powerful. They cause pain for the addicts and for those who love them. When you love someone, you don't want to see them in pain, so you try to "make it better". You can't. First of all, It's not your job to fix someone else's life. It's theirs to handle. People all have two choices in this matter. You can live your lives embracing your addictions, which isn't truly living at all - or you can give up your addictions for only one day at a time. You can continue your addictions tomorrow, but just for one day, don't fall back into your addicted compulsive behavior pattern. It's only for one day. That's all the human body and brain can handle. Then you can become free for just one day at a time and it feels so good. One day will then turn into two, and then hundreds and thousands of days. It's a wonderful strategy to remember ... One day at a time."

"I want you to know something very important. Everyone is encased in a beautiful rainbow Bubble of Love and Light which is God's love for you. What you bring into your Bubble of Love is yours to keep and release at any time.

You can bring in love, peace, and hope, or you can bring in old tired beliefs, pain, fear, and worry. You can also bring in drugs, alcohol, cigarettes, people-pleasing, and whatever you choose. You are in your Bubble of Love, and everyone else has their bubble. This Bubble of Love is a divine gift from God and it is sacred territory. This bubble is your LIFE and you are free to add or subtract whatever you wish at any time. You have control over whatever is in your Bubble of Love. Your POWER lies inside the sacred space of your Bubble of Love. Problems arise when others leave their bubble and enter your bubble uninvited, or if you leave to enter another's bubble uninvited. Only one person per bubble, please! There is no room in a bubble for more than one. Your sacred bubble recognizes your energy. If another's energy enters your Bubble of Love it results in drama and negativity. Now you can understand that although you wanted to "fix me", you could not, and you knew that. Mom, we all need to stay in our Bubble of Love because the energy there will be exclusively ours, and that's the only way we will be able to sort out a lot of things. We can take in what we need, and rid ourselves of what we no longer need or want. False ideas and old beliefs that aren't true anymore must go. That's why we don't want anyone else's energy gunking up our bubble energy. I know you understand now why nobody can be fixed. The only person you can fix is yourself. You couldn't help me, Mom. So you can't go on a guilt trip. Throw guilt out of your bubble right now, Ma. Guilt and shame don't belong in your bubble anymore. You were never responsible for what I kept in my bubble. Kapeesh? Clean out your bubble, Ma, and tell everyone to stay in their own Bubble of Love. Take care to manage your own bubble and leave the management of others' bubbles to those who reside there. I send light and love to all and tell you that it's all good."

"Thanks, Marc. You said it all. I understand, but I am so used to putting myself on a guilt trip for not being everything to everybody. We moms are great at doing that, you know. It's hell being a mom and wanting to fix everyone's suffering. To have a MOM HEART is a daunting and complicated experience. We love so deeply. But I wouldn't trade it for the world. Even though I have the love of Adam and Denny and his kids, after you crossed over I felt like a body without a heart. Without a soul. An empty shell. My energy had left me. But, by talking to you, I am starting to see between the lines in this process of grieving. It takes time, and we have a lot of questions. Thanks for clearing up some stuff for me. It's helping me let go of a ton of pain. I love you."

"It's all good, Ma. Remember, I get it... I've been a mother before. I love you, too. You're doing fine, sweet Mama. One day at a time. You've got this!"

MARCH 15, 2022

Here we go again!! Andie called me today and told me that she went online to order a product from the TV home shopping network. She put it in her cart and went to check out. She noticed that the cost of the order came to double what she thought it should be. She went back to check to make sure she hadn't ordered two of the item. Oh, she had only ordered one, but there was another item in her cart. In her cart - are you ready for this? - was a goat milk five-piece moisturizer and lotion set. Seriously?? Are you kidding me? She had not put that in her cart! We both knew who did it!! She got "Carked" again. (Honey, ya gotta stop doing that. Now we know how Andie's daughter got *her* goat milk gift!!). I know how much you love to give presents, Cark! You're too much!

MARCH 22, 2022

Tonight we did a video group reading with a bunch of our psychic medium gals. Marc seems to be the Spirit Guide for this group, as his energy always comes in. We were reading for a sister of one of the gals, and one of the mediums gave her evidence of loved ones who have crossed over ("she likes to eat spaghetti, but no other kind of pasta", and "his shoestrings were always untied". Stuff like that to give evidence of a loved-one presence). Then this medium said that she saw a tall, dark-bearded man come in. He was happy and he sat with his hands back behind his head and he was laughing. The lady we read for could not connect with that energy. It's okay when that happens because it might not be for them, or it might be something that they can connect with later. Anyway, we all continued to read cards and call in departed loved ones. It was a lovely reading. When the lady who had the reading left the video call, the rest of us mediums discussed how we thought it went. At the end of that conversation, I asked the medium who saw the tall, dark-bearded man if she thought that man might be my son. Andie was there, and she said she got "goosebumps and chills" when I mentioned my son. She laughed and said that it was Marc hanging around with the "Old Fart Mediums". He loves us and always wants to be with us. He's too much. He just walked right into the middle of a reading. Just strolled right on in! We've been "Carked" for sure!

MARCH 25, 2022

This morning Marc told me, *"I came out like a peacock struttin' my stuff."* Oh?? Okay?? Whatever??? I didn't know why he told me that, but he did. I watched the weather channel this afternoon, and the meteorologist told everyone that today was National Peacock Day. Holy smokes! Are you serious? I can't make this stuff up! Marc, you're too much. Keep your fun ways. They brighten my day and make me laugh, and laughter is the best medicine. Shake a tail feather, baby!

MARCH 26, 2022

Marc is still sending us rainbows on cloudy days. Blows my mind. Each rainbow makes my heart so grateful that he is sending us love and telling us that he is at peace.

MARCH 27, 2022

We live in an apartment building where people are always moving in or out. Sometimes good furniture and accessories or kitchen items are left behind. Today, Denny called me to our front door. Outside of our apartment, next to the main entrance, was a square, black, side table with a white piece of paper taped to the top. On the paper was written the word "FREE" ... and a smiley face was under that word. The smiley face looked exactly like the one Marc would always make, and it did indeed look like Marc had written the note. <u>THAT NOTE WAS IN MARC'S HANDWRITING</u>. Both Denny and I were amazed! We just stared at it and shook our heads. I brought the table inside and sent Reiki energy to clear it and I now use it next to my recliner. (Marc knew that I needed a table, and the funny thing is that a couple of weeks ago, I put out into the Universe that I needed a table next to my recliner.... God always provides!!!). I removed the note and taped it to our counter where I could see it always. It brings me such joy. MARC IS FREE!

Joy Elaine Reed

CHAPTER 25

THE ORANGE DETOUR

APRIL 4, 2022

Denny and I had business to attend to, so we drove across the blue bridge over the river to a lovely little town which is our county seat. It's so beautiful there, with a town square and a large white gazebo in the grassy green space in the center of town. It's a nice walking town with a little main street, and I feel good there. It was a sunny, cool spring day that made me feel alive. The dirty, brown snow had finally melted from the sides of the roads. Seeing the blooming tulips and blossoming crab-apple trees delighted me and brought joy to my heart. The earth is finally waking up and putting on fancy clothes YAY!! Thank you, Lord. I enjoyed seeing the sights of this new season because winter had been so damn long and dreary. The darkness of the winter was turning into light, and blooming surprises. After we had our meeting, I came out of the building and took off my mask, and inhaled a deep breath of fragrant springtime air. The fresh air smelled so good to me. I noticed an ornamental cherry tree next to the front door. I'm a tree girl. Trees are part of my tribe. I walked up to this gorgeous tree and noticed that she had buds on her limbs… they were tight but they were ready to burst open any day now. They were pale pink with darker pink tips. They looked like big pink kernels of popcorn ready to pop. I touched her supple branches. She was breathtakingly beautiful and as I felt her softness, the enchantment of springtime filled my energy centers. It was such a sweet experience, feeling the good energy of springtime. I wished that Marc were here to witness our world colorfully exploding into spring, and I started to cry and sob because I missed him. I sobbed as I walked down the parking lot to the car. My babe, Denny, understands and he handed me a tissue. I just miss Marc so much and wanted him with me at this most beautiful time of year. He appreciated all of nature and felt at home outdoors. I wished he were here in the sunshine with us to see the buds on the trees, even though I know he can see the buds on the trees anytime he wants. I just miss him. He's been living at his new address for the past year and a half.

I cried my way through town. I cried because spring here is so lovely, and because Marc has crossed over. I was happy and sad at the same time. I was feeling my sadness and I allowed it to come to the surface so I could let it go. On the main street, we stopped at a red light by the cemetery. I looked up and saw a sign that I had never seen before. It was on the road next to the new crypts they are building in the cemetery. This sign was a large orange and white sign that read "Orange Detour" and had an arrow on it that pointed up. In all my years, I had never seen a sign like that before. Because it was big and orange, and next to a cemetery, I knew it had something to do with Marc!! Marc, what's with this sign? Are you trying to tell me something?

That night, before I fell asleep, I heard Marc tell me... *"Hey, Ma, I want you to know that some souls take detours when they return home. I have taken the Orange Detour on my journey, but it still got me where I needed to go and where we're all going to end up. That's what a detour is all about, it's just an alternate route that brings you to the place where you're ultimately headed. It doesn't matter which way you go. We all take different routes. Whether we take a detour or not, we'll all end up in the same place and we'll all be together one day. It will be a beautiful homecoming. Life goes on.*

Souls come and go. Some take the main roads, some take side streets, some take alleys, some take freeways and some take detours. It doesn't matter, our destination is always in view. I am finally where I belong."

"*Our souls will live forever. Relax and enjoy. Just do what you need to do in your life and then it will be time to move on. Remember, only your life is yours to live. Enjoy life… it is a sacred gift. It is filled with love energy to carry with you everywhere you go. Have fun, and experience to the max everything that is good and loving. Live your life in such a way that you will be a blessing to others. Then you will bring those blessings with you into eternity. Shine your light, Ma. When you live a good life filled with love, it brings joy to all of us here in the Afterlife. I wish you love, Mom. Love is everything. Anything else is just an illusion. All is love, and love is all.*"

This is the journey Marc took.
I love that the arrow points upward!

CHAPTER 26

IT'S ALL GOOD

APRIL 5, 2022

I poured a cup of coffee, pulled out a chair, and sat at the table waiting to get last night's sleep out of my head. My thoughts went to Marc - how much I miss him, and how the world is a better place because he was and is here. I thought about how surprised I was to see the "Orange Detour" sign that he showed me yesterday on our way home. That sign from him let me know that his entire Birthing-into-Spirit Journey is now over. He's now totally safe in a place of peace, joy, bliss, and unconditional love. He is free.

I had been wondering about the book's ending, and I had been praying for Spirit to help me tie the loose strings together. I knew that Marc would come through to me when the time was right, and apparently, this morning was a perfect time. Marc had a lot to tell me and he wanted me to share this with you…

"Ma, before I was ever born, when I was in a different time and place, I picked you especially to be my mother because I knew that you would be the one woman with the strength to write my story and give hope to others. You gave birth to me, and through you, I gave birth to this book. This book has finally been written, but we'll never be finished…"

"I wanted you especially to be my mother because you were always able to see the big picture. You saw through life's illusions and understood what truly mattered. You

understood that all is love. And, you're absolutely right! That's how it is here, Mom. We see everything clearly now that we are free from the bodies that we had carried around on the earth plane. We now have high-frequency energy bodies of love. It's all love here. Here we see things in love's light. We have no time for drama. We have no time for judgment. We have no time for sorrow. We have no time for pain. We have no time for resentment. All that has dropped away and is gone. Everything here unfolds as it should at the perfect time. It's all good."

"I see you cry. I see your pain. I know that you are crying for yourself, Mom… not for me. You feel abandoned. I did not abandon you. It was my time to come home. I am happy that you realize that I am in a better place - much better than your place where there is so much suffering. Mom, there is no suffering here. We are all free! Write that in your journal and then write HALLELUJAH."

"You must grieve. It is a necessary and important process. There is nothing I can do to help you just like there was nothing you could do to help me when I was there on earth. All I can do is reassure you. Time is healing your heart because I notice you don't cry so deeply and so often anymore. I am happy to see you healing. The rainbows I send are symbols of hope. I am so glad that you listen to my voice and notice all the signs and messages that I give you. I do my best to provide comfort to you and remind you that I will be with you always. I love you. Remember me happy."

"Death is only a quiet passage downstream in the flow of life. We whom you call "dead" are all still very much alive. Our souls' experiences have no abrupt endings. Death doesn't stop our journey down the stream. We continue on and the stream grows wider. The water is crystal clear. Rocks and rapids are nowhere to be seen and cease being a threat to us. Nothing can threaten us here. We cannot be hurt because we are safe. We flow effortlessly down the stream

into the shining pure light of love that continually surrounds us. We don't need to try to paddle upstream like you do when you live on the earth plane. Here we just go with the flow."

"Where we are, there is only bliss. Peace comes to all of us when we leave our earthly bodies and our souls are exposed to the light of Spirit's love. Suffering is over and our souls are released from all the pain that our mortal bodies held. Ma, I wish you could know how light I feel! I am love, in a place of love, with beings of love! You have felt this bliss before, Mom, and you know that it is real."

"Let death hold no fear for you. Death is nothing but a word that we use while we are in our bodies because souls on the earthly plane think and speak in words. "Death" is just a word you say when the soul leaves the body to move on. But, when the body is gone we become free! So "death" should be a word of encouragement, not an image of pain and sadness. Celebrate! We have been reborn into Spirit!"

"Where I am now there is no need for words… we "know". That's what death truly is - a trip into "knowing". It's a new birth into knowing. Knowing compassion, knowing the truth, knowing pure love. Here we all are happy, joyous, and free."

"Mom, live the best life you can. Relax, enjoy, and laugh. Forgive and hold no resentments. Have no judgments and no regrets. Do not worry. Be kind. Live a full life. Give, give, give, and then give some more. Dance! Sing! Celebrate your soul!"

"Think of me often, Ma. Remember the fun side of me. Talk to me while you're eating dinner. Laugh at the crazy memories that we made together. Celebrate my birthday and sing! Keep an eye out for continuing signs that I am with you. If you see somebody that looks like me - it is me! Know that I am always near. Keep looking for the rainbows and signs that I send you, they will continue to bring you hope forever."

"Be happy for me, Mom. I am surrounded by love and I am love. I am more alive now than I have ever been before. It's all good. I am in the "Utopian Society" that you wrote about in your journal. I made it to that place of ultimate loving-kindness. Ma, I don't miss you because I am always with you. We are soulmates who will forever be together in our voyage through eternity. Hold that truth in your heart, Mom. Death is just a word. I am not gone! Shout that out to Adam, Brittany, Dad, Denny, and everybody in the world! I am all the glowing stars in the night sky winking at you. I am all the birds who sing their sweet songs of gratitude every morning. I am the unending and evolving Universe. I am all the colors of the rainbows that you love."

"Thanks for writing the book, Mom! I knew you could do it. Ma, you and I were assigned to give hope. The people who are meant to read this book WILL read this book. Spirit has already taken care of that."

"Mom, if the messages and signs that I have sent you from the Hereafter, and that you have shared, have given just one person on earth the strength to face their fears… then we're batting a thousand! If my Afterlife messages and signs have given just one person on earth the determination to stop using drugs or quit their addictions and wake up to the love of a higher power… then we've earned the blue ribbon! If my messages and signs from the Beyond have given just one person on earth the courage to be their authentic self and to come out to their family and friends… then we're running on a full tank of gas! If my messages and signs from the Afterlife have given just one person on earth the inspiration to adopt an attitude of loving-kindness… then we've won the gold medal! And, if we have changed the life of just one person on earth and have given them hope… then, Mom, we have accomplished our divine purpose! We only need to help one person heal, Mom! Just ONE!"

"The book is now complete and I thank you because I couldn't have done this without you. I thank you for being so brave and for carrying out the work of Spirit."

"As for this book… don't write "The End", Ma. There is no end. Our story and our souls will go on forever. Think "Eternity", Mom. "Love For Eternity" is where I am and who I am. I am with you and I am everywhere but I am not gone. Spirit sent me on the Orange Detour to the Afterlife because it was my time to leave. Eventually, we will all end up in the same place. In time we will all be together again."

"I love you eternally, Mom, and I'll be here to meet you when you return Home."

Joy Elaine Reed

The love between a mother and her son knows no distance.

Made in the USA
Monee, IL
25 May 2023